Handcrafted Fashion Art from Japan

wagashi

Kumiko Sudo

Breckling Press

Library of Congress Cataloging-in-Publication Data
Sudo, Kumiko.
  Wagashi : handcrafted fashion art from japan / Kumiko Sudo.
     p. cm.
  1. Fashion drawing--Japan. 2. Fashion design--Japan. I. Title.

TT509.S855 2007
741.6'72--dc22

2007016356
This book was set in Guardi, Helvetica Neue Ultra Light and Lichten
Editorial direction by Anne Knudsen
Calligraphy and watercolor paintings by Kumiko Sudo
Design and production by Maria Mann
Cover and interior photographs by Sharon Hoogstraten
Technical drawings by Eliza Wheeler

My heartfelt thanks to friends and students in Japan who
have generously shared their kimono fabrics.

Published by Breckling Press
283 N. Michigan St, Elmhurst, IL 60126
Printed and bound in China
International Standard Book Number (ISBN 13): 978-1-933308-14-2
International Standard Book Number (ISBN 10): 1-933308-14-1

Dedication

To my mother, who taught me so much

Contents

Namagashi

Yokan

A Little Something Sweet

和菓子

Every visitor to Japan soon learns the meaning of the word *wagashi*. Wagashi are those delightfully sweet and beautifully designed confections that are always offered alongside a refreshing cup of tea, or in an prettily wrapped box as a parting gift. Crafted by skilled artisans, wagashi come in an endless and beautiful variety, from delicately patterned dry candies to jellied sweets molded into wondrous shapes.

For this book, I translate *wagashi* to mean "sweet little things." They are hand-made treasures, so exquisitely crafted that they make our eyes light up with pleasure when we see them. On closer inspection, we discover delicate details and pretty embellishments that deepen our delight. I hope that you enjoy the various projects in this book, which are intended as gifts for those you love. Even more, I wish you the joy of seeing how much happiness these "sweet little things" can bring to the friends who receive them.

Kumiko Sudo

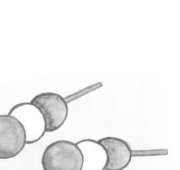

A Guide to Technique

In *Wagashi* you will find twenty-two small projects.
The book title is inspired by the delicate and
masterfully designed candies that are often served
with tea in Japan. I like to think of *wagashi* as
art-in-miniature; they are so prettily and carefully
constructed that they are invariably admired
before they are consumed. In fact, many people
in Japan collect and save *wagashi*—they are
often considered too pretty to eat!

作り方の案内

The projects in my *Wagashi* collection are meant to arouse the same pleasurable feelings. Created to be made and given as gifts, there are exquisite necklaces, elegant braided bracelets, pretty pins, and several small totes and purses—all delightful, intimate fashion accessories. Like Japanese *wagashi* candies, they have been designed with inordinate care; it is my hope that they will bring the same sense of joy that I experience each time I open a new box of *wagashi*.

As you browse through this book, you will see that some projects incorporate familiar materials and techniques that I have used in my earlier collections. As before, I have chosen Japanese silks, American cottons, and soft, natural-woven felts to construct several of the items. For the first time, I introduce some lovely *kumihimo* braiding techniques that are popular in Japan; while at first glace, some of my braided jewelry may seem complex, you will soon find that a little practice will allow you to achieve the same patterns and effects you see in the photographs. Several projects include beading and embroidery. I encourage you to seek out unusual embellishments to add to your projects, making each gift you give unique and personal. Some of the projects are very simple and can be completed in less than an hour. *Bugaku* on page 26, *Suzu Mari* on page 102 and, of course, my fabric

Sewing Kit

Wagashi is designed as a collection of take-along projects, requiring only basic sewing tools that will fit easily into a small tote. A materials list is supplied with each project. In addition, keep the following items close to hand.

Hand-sewing needles	Cotton stuffing or batting scraps	Tailor's chalk or non-permanent marker
Embroidery needles (large eye)	Thread snips	Ruler
Pins and pincushion	Fabric scissors	Flexible tape measure
Thimble	Paper scissors	Toothpick or dollmaker's awl
Quality threads in a variety of colors	Sharp pencils	Hooks and eyes
Quality embroidery floss in a variety of colors	Eraser	Snap fasteners

thimbles on page 132 are easy to make. Simple purses, like *Periwinkle* on page 84 and *Malipoense Pouch* on page 124 introduce fabric-origami flowers and can be completed in a day. Other projects, such as the more challenging *Hana-Chiru-Sato* necklace on page 46 or *Protea* on page 18 take more time and patience, yet these are the ones that will give you the most pleasure.

Fabrics

The projects in *Wagashi* present you with a wonderful opportunity to showcase special fabrics. Many of the samples photographed are crafted from Japanese silks, *shiboris*, or *chiromen* crepe; other are made from beautifully designed and readily available contemporary cottons. For years, I have collected traditional Japanese textiles and I now have a large selection of antique kimono and obi. I have cut up several of them in order to incorporate their rich colors and patterns into my designs. I save each scrap, no matter how small, to make small gifts like the ones in this book. As I am writing this book, I am also busy designing the second series of my own line of fabrics. The first

series, *Cho Cho no Sanpomichi* (*Flight of the Butterfly*) is produced by *In the Beginning* fabric company, based in Seattle. Of course, as I create the fabric designs, I imagine all kinds of small projects that I will be able to make from small swatches or scraps. My fabric designs may be a good choice for you, too.

To make the designs in *Wagashi*, you do not need to have a large fabric collection, nor do you need to spend a lot of money. The projects are intended to be made from small scraps and you can easily mix and match fabrics within a single design. For this reason, I have not specified exact yardages for any of the projects. Even for some of the larger purses, you will need no more than a sixteenth of a yard of any particular fabric. If you are shopping for new fabrics, I suggest you buy ⅛ yard of every fabric that catches your eye and ¼ yard of those that are irresistible. This way, you will have enough fabric for two, three, or more of the projects you are making. Look for a variety of colors and shades, and try to find some fabrics with strong motifs that you will be able to highlight in a pleasing way. Using the photographs as a guide to contrast, I suggest you select colors and patterns that you enjoy the most. It is the combinations you choose that will make your gifts unique.

Working with Felts

Many of the projects in *Wagashi* incorporate felt. Soft to the touch, I particularly like to use felt as the lining for purses and for the backing of jewelry. With a felt backing, necklaces

and bracelets float gracefully on the skin, and they are com-
fortable to wear all day. Precious items slipped inside felt-lined
purses remain safe and scratch-free. Quality felts are available
by the yard from several companies. I particularly like the all-
natural wool felts from National Nonwovens. They come in
rich textures and a variety of luxurious colors. Avoid pre-cut
craft felts, which are usually rough to the touch and may bleed
upon exposure to damp or perspiration.

Quality felt is a delight to sew. Since it doesn't fray, there
is no need for hemming. It holds even the smallest stitches
securely. Use matching-color thread and your stitches will
sink into the felt and become invisible. For several of the small
pouches and totes in *Wagashi*, I slip pieces of felt inside the
outer fabric, giving the project a soft, padded feel.

Cutting

Full-size templates are provided for all pieces other than simple
squares, circles, and rectangles. If you plan on making several
of the projects in *Wagashi*, I recommend that you make templates of these basic shapes from template plastic or stiff card.
This will save you the trouble of measuring and drawing new
shapes each time you need one. See page 135 for help on making templates.

Read the pattern and the template pieces carefully to make
sure you allow the correct seam allowance for each piece. Most

purse pieces, for instance, require a generous ½″ seam allow-ance, while templates for smaller projects use ¼″ or even ⅛″ seam allowances. For circles, squares, and rectangles, the seam allowance is already included in the measurement provided. Felt, used as lining or padding for several projects, requires no seam allowance at all. Since the templates are all quite small and multiples of the same piece are rarely needed, I use sharp scissors rather than rotary cutting equipment. Whichever method you use, remember to transfer any markings from the pattern onto the cut pieces of fabric.

Sewing

I sew everything—straight seams and curved seams, piecing and appliqué—by hand. When I sew, I feel my hands are direct-ed by my heart and I like the sense of intimacy that hand-sewing gives me. I am particularly sensitive to this emotion when I am making gifts. Since all the projects in *Wagashi* are quite small, you may want to sew them by hand, too. If you prefer to sew by machine, you will find that straight seams, such as the side seams in most of the purse projects, turn out beautifully. In certain projects, however, where you may need to manipulate the fabric as you sew, you may find that hand-sewing is not only faster, but more accurate.

Many of the designs involve sewing curved seams. For per-fect curved seams, I use a form of appliqué or invisible stitching that is described below. My technique involves placing a fabric piece, with the seam allowance folded under, on top of a background piece; the piece is then blind-stitched by hand. In the instructions, this is what is meant by the term *appliqué*. The term *sew* indicates a more traditional method of sewing the pieces together, right sides facing, using a running stitch on the wrong side of the seam lines. Straight seams are sewn in this way, and you may use hand or machine stitching.

Appliqué Stitches

The appliqué technique I use to attach appliqués of flowers, leaves, or stems onto my projects result in tiny stiches that are not visible from the front. The appliqués lie flat, for a smooth, clean effect.

1. Fold under the seam allowance of the appliqué and press or finger-press it firmly. Pin the appliqué in place through the seam allowance onto the background fabric.

2. Insert the needle through a single thread in the weave of background fabric. As soon as it emerges from the fabric, re-insert the needle into the appliqué at the fold line. Exit at a point ¼" further along the fold line. This will neatly hide the knot in the folded seam allowance.

3. Repeat, pulling the thread firmly with each stich. In effect, the thread is hidden in the "tunnel" inside the folded seam allowance of the appliqué.

If you are working with slippery fabrics like silks or with small appliqués, it is helpful to baste the seam allowance of the appliqué firmly in place before beginning the appliqué stitch. This will prevent distortion of the fabric. Take care to fold over any tips or sharp corners precisely before basting. Remove the basting stitches once the appliqué is in place.

Fabric Origami

Many of the projects in *Wagashi* incorporate fabric origami, or the folding of fabric to create new shapes. The flowers that embellish *Periwinkle Pinwheel* on page 84 and *Hana-Chiru-Sato* on page 46 are folded from simple shapes.

A key difference between folding paper and folding fabric is that paper is available with different colors on the two sides. To achieve the same effect with fabric, you must first sew the two colors of your choice together, then turn them right side out and press. Often, finger pressing will be adequate.

Preparing Flower Shapes

All the origami flower designs begin with a simple shape—a circle, a square, or a pentagon. Use the same steps to prepare all shapes, as follows. All flower templates already include a ¼" seam allowance.

1. Using the templates indicated in the pattern you have selected, cut the fabrics as needed and arrange the shapes into

pairs. Take care to achieve good color contrast between the fabrics in each pair.

2. Matching contrasting colors (light to dark) and right sides together, sew the pairs together by hand or by machine around the outer edges, leaving a 2″ opening.

3. Fold the seams inward toward the center of the shape and press. If you are preparing a circle, follow the curved line to make a nice, rounded curve. For angled shapes, poke a toothpick or dollmaker's awl into the angles to assure crisp corners. Turn the shape right side out, then blind-stitch the opening closed. Lightly press to reinforce the shape.

Just as in traditional paper origami, which uses paper decorated in different colors and patterns on either side, you now have a two-sided shape to begin folding your flowers.

Even if you know nothing of traditional Japanese origami, you will find that my fabric-folding techniques are easy to learn. These tips may help

- Study each folding diagram carefully before you begin. Determine which is the right and wrong side of the fabric. Go through the step-by-step instructions mentally before you even pick up the fabric. You may find it helpful to practice each new shape on a sample so that you solve any difficulties before you begin your final piece.

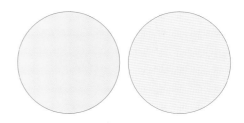

Step 1

Step 2

Step 3

- Always fold accurately and neatly.

- Crease each fold firmly with the back of your thumbnail. Good creases make the folding easier, and they serve as guides to future steps.

You will find that the same procedures are used over and over again. You will soon become so proficient with them that you can carry them out almost without thinking.

Beading

I have always loved beads and enjoy incorporating them into my sewing. Almost all of the projects in *Wagashi* are embellished with beads. Beading is simple and does not take much time or practice, yet it lends a wonderful new dimension to jewelry or fashion accessories.

Types of Beads

Today, there is an incredible variety of beads available from specialty bead stores, catalogs, and web sites. Crafts stores also carry beautiful selections. Because the projects in *Wagashi* are small scale, I tend to choose small beads. I particularly enjoy highlighting the beautiful patterns I find in fabric with delicate placement of seed beads. My favorites are Japanese delica beads (size 11—the larger the size number, the smaller the bead), which are tiny cylinders, no more than 2 mm long. They come is an amazing variety of colors and finishes. Delicas are easy to sew, lying flat against the fabric and adding texture, dimension, and shine. *Evening Primrose* on page 116, is just one of the projects that feature delicas. Tiny daisy patterns made from delicas embellish my otherwise plain thimbles on page 132. I sometimes use Czech seed beads, which have a more rounded shape, in place of delicas. I also like longer cylinder beads, such as 3 mm delicas (size 8). Bugle beads are another favorite. These longer cylinders come in a variety of lengths. *Hagoromo* on page 128 features ¾" bugles.

I use small round beads both for sewing directly onto projects, as in *Berry, Berry* on page 40, and, more often, to string onto embroidery floss, then allow them to dangle. Depending on the scale of the project, they may measure anywhere from 3 mm to 6 mm. On occasion, I allow beads to be a focal point of a design and choose beautiful lampwork beads, like the one on *Protea* on page 18. It is fun to spend an hour or two in a specialty store to find beads that will be perfect for your sewing projects. If you do not have a good store in your area, devote a couple of hours to searching beading web sites—and then look forward to your packages of beautiful beads arriving in the mail.

Sewing Beads

While there are specialty threads available from bead stores, designed for sewing beads, I tend to use a strong, high-quality hand-sewing thread or embroidery floss. I use a simple running stitch to sew seed beads or small round beads in place. Sometimes, I follow the design in the fabric or follow the shape of a particular template; other times I place beads to reflect the veins of a leaf, as in *Periwinkle Pinweel* shown here. My technique is always the same—a simple running stitch that neatly hides the thread.

I secure larger beads by stitching through them two or three times. Sometimes it is necessary to "lock" beads in place, using a small bead or seed bead. I simply stack the desired beads, then run the thread through them as shown. The tiny bead on top locks the others in place. The thread goes through the first and second beads, then through one side of the seed bead and out the other, and back down into the other two beads.

Stringing beads for purse handles or for jewelry that dangles is easy and fun. Knot a strand of two-ply embroidery floss or heavy-duty sewing thread. Make a stitch to secure it at the spot where the handle starts. String beads in the desired pattern, then make a double stitch at the point where the handle ends.

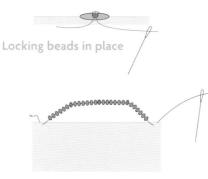

Simple running stitch

Locking beads in place

String beads for purse handle

Embroidery

Adding embroidery is a simple and delicate way to add subtle highlights to your sewing projects. For the projects in *Wagashi*, there is no need to master a variety of stitches. A few key skills that require minimal practice are all you need.

Herringbone Stitch

I use two-ply embroidery floss and a simple herringbone stitch to sew together the fronts and backs of several of the purses and pouches in *Wagashi*. You can see a simple herringbone stitch along the edge of the pin cushion shown here. When working on a purse, pin the front and back together, aligning any curves. Hide the knot on the inside of the purse, on the bottom layer of fabric, exiting the needle at the front. Draw the thread upwards and diagonally to the right, then make a small stitch into the top layer of fabric. The needle exits immediately to the left of its entry point. Draw the thread downwards and diagonally to the left, then make a tiny stitch in the bottom layer of fabric, again exiting the needle immediately to the left of its entry point. Continue to the end, then make a double stitch to secure.

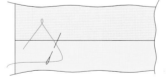

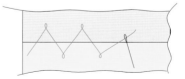

Kumihimo Braiding

Most of the lovely jewelry projects and some of the purses in *Wagashi* include *kumihimo*, which is the Japanese word for braiding with specialty cords. Some of the projects are braided with embroidery floss, others with macramé cord, and still others with novelty yarns and cords, available from craft and yarn stores. Beading stores and web sites are another good source for quality braiding cords. (See page 151 for a list of helpful resources.)

For each project that includes braiding, detailed instructions are provided. Here are some general guidelines to help make your braids as perfect and as beautiful as they can be.

- Always buy high-quality braiding materials. Braiding demands time and patience; if you invest in top quality cords and threads, your work will be truly rewarded.

- Check for colorfastness. Test every cord or thread by washing a small sample in warm water. Rinse in cold water to make sure that no color runs out. If the cord still bleeds color after two or three rinses, do not use it in your projects. With jewelry, in particular, avoid non-colorfast materials; the least perspiration may spoil the piece.

- When working with multiple cords or threads, it is easy to lose track. To avoid mistakes, label each thread at the end of the strand; simply wrap the end in tape and label it A, B, C, etc., corresponding to the drawings that accompany each braiding project.

- For tight braids like *Evening Primrose* bracelet on page 118, tug hard on each strand of cord or floss after every knot. For loose braids such as *Purple Dianthus* on page 78, tug gently but firmly, allowing a little space between each knot.

- While my instructions provide approximate yard lengths to cut for each braid, always allow a little extra length before cutting your cord or floss.

- When your braids are complete, dab a little fabric glue over the finishing knot as a safeguard against fraying.

- Practice, practice, practice. Before you start on each project, cut some shorter sample threads to practice each braiding technique or knot.

Manju

The magical ingredient of those soft, sticky cakes known as *manju* is the modest *azuki* bean. In the hands of a Japanese candy artisan, this soft, pliable, and deliciously sweet red bean works up into a miraculous paste that can be swiftly molded into a variety of shapes. A little powdered sugar on top, and the treat is complete. The projects in this chapter, handcrafted from fabrics and felts, will bring you a similar sensation of sweet satisfaction.

"This sweet but sophisticated purse makes an elegant fashion statement. The burst of color against a dark background reminds me of a bright hibiscus greeting the morning."

Protea

During a visit to Egypt, I stayed at a hotel that had a courtyard surrounded by hibiscus trees in full bloom. Hundreds of little birds flittered in and out of the vivid red protea or hibiscus flowers, warbling their songs. I would hear them each morning as I awoke, refreshed for the day ahead. In designing this purse, I combined the memory of my trip with images from ancient Egypt. The black background fabric with the arabesque pattern is silk. I placed the hibiscus flower in the middle, and below it is a moon and star taken from some antique earrings.

Make one flower

1. Make a circle template measuring 4½" diameter, then cut two from fabric. Follow the directions on page 8 to prepare the circles for folding. Mark the center of the circle.

Selections

Purse fabric: ⅛ yard or less of cotton or silk in two contrasting colors

Lining fabric: ⅛ yard or less of cotton or silk

Padding: Felt scraps

Flower and stems: Scraps of cotton (four or five colors)

Beads: Large decorative bead or button

Braiding cord: About 4 yards

#25 embroidery floss (6-ply)

Snap fastener

See templates A and B on page 136. Use ½" seam allowance for purse pieces only; use ¼" seam allowance for other sewing.

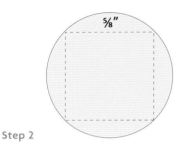

5/8"

Step 2

Step 4

2. Turn in each side by 5/8", then press firmly to mark a 2½" square, as shown by the dashed lines in the diagram. Open out.

3. Make a circle template measuring 2" diameter, then cut nine (one circle from a bright color for the flower center, plus four circles each from two other fabrics). Position the bright circle at the center of the square and baste it in place.

4. Fold the remaining eight circles in half and press. Fold twice more as shown, making a petal shape. Pin to hold.

5. Position then pin all eight petals inside the press-lines of the square as shown, spacing them evenly to fill the square. With a continuous thread, stitch all eight petals in place, hiding the raw edge of the center circle.

6. Fold the curved edges of the circle inwards to form a perfect square and stitch in place, hiding the raw edges of the petals.

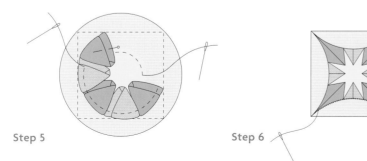

Step 5

Step 6

Back view

Make the purse

7. With templates A and B, cut two each from felt (be sure to place A on the fold of the fabric before cutting). Add ½" seam allowance to the templates, then cut two more of each from your selections of outer fabric plus two each from lining fabric. Transfer the dashed line on template B onto the fronts of the fabric pieces. Cut two strips of felt measuring 1¼" × 4", and two strips of fabric measuring 3" × 5".

8. Fold in ½" seam allowances on outer purse fabric pieces A and B. Press to hold. Slip a corresponding felt piece inside the folded-in seam allowance of each piece. Sew the felt to the folded-in seam allowance, taking care not to let the needle go through to the fabric front.

9. Making sure the seam allowances are folded inwards and pressed, position lining pieces A and B from step 7, wrong sides together, over the corresponding pieces from step 8. Use overcast stitch to sew in place, hiding the turned-in seam allowances and the felt padding.

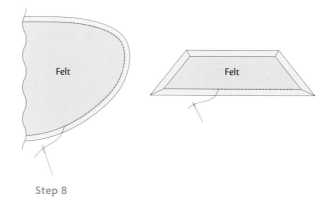

Felt

Felt

Step 8

Step 10

Step 11

10. For the stems, cut four strips of fabric measuring $\frac{5}{8}$" × 7". Cut on the bias to give the stems a little extra stretch. Fold in a $\frac{1}{8}$" seam allowance. Position the stems on the completed purse front piece from step 9, curving them as shown in the photograph. Pin and then appliqué each stem in place.

11. Position a felt strip from step 7 on top of a fabric strip, as shown. Fold in a $\frac{1}{2}$" seam allowance around all edges of the fabric strip. Stitch the folded-in seam allowance to the felt along both sides and the bottom edge. Fold the top edge over, completely hiding the felt, and use overcast stitch to sew in place. In the same way, stitch up both sides. Repeat with the second set of strips. Set aside.

12. Position a completed piece A from step 10 so that the top curve sits on the marked line on piece B. Appliqué along the entire curve, attaching A to B. Next, position this piece on top of the padded strip from step 11, so that it overlaps the strip by about ½". Appliqué in place, completing the purse front. Repeat for the purse back. Sew the flower from step 1 to the purse front, as shown in the photograph.

13. For the side panel, cut a strip of fabric measuring 2" × 17" and a strip of felt measuring ¾" × 16". As in step 11, fold in a ½" seam allowance around all sides of the fabric piece, then wrap the felt inside the fabric and stitch to hide the felt padding.

14. Using a 2-ply strand of embroidery floss and herringbone stitch (see page 13), sew the side panel first to the front, then to the back, working from the top and working evenly around the entire curve of piece A.

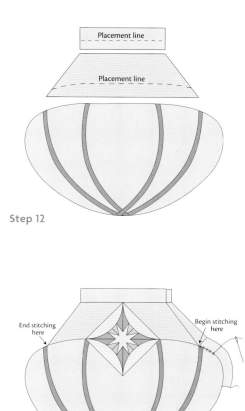

Placement line

Placement line

Step 12

End stitching here

Begin stitching here

Step 14

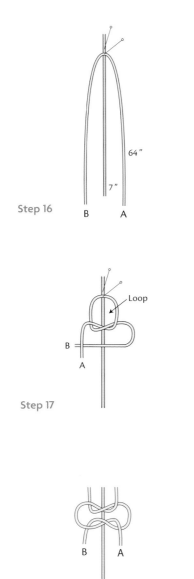

64"

7"

Step 16   B   A

Loop

B

A

Step 17

B   A

Step 18

Weave two square-knot handles

15. For each handle, cut a length of cord measuring 7" (core cord) and a length measuring 64" (weaving cord). Note that the core cord will be completely hidden by the braid.

16. Pin the core cord to a firm pincushion or corkboard, about 1" from the end. Fold the weaving cord in half, then pin the midpoint on top of the core cord, pushing this second pin through both cords.

17. Pick up the right-hand weaving cord (A) and loop it *under* the core cord, then *over* the left-hand weaving cord (B). Hold in place with your thumb. Pick up B and weave it *over* the core cord, then down through the loop, as shown. Pull the ends of the weaving cords to close up the loops and complete the first half-square knot.

18. Pick up the right-hand weaving cord (B) and loop it *over* the core cord, then *under* the left-hand weaving cord (A). Hold in place with your thumb. Pick up A and weave it *under* the core cord, then up through the loop. As before, pull to close the loops and complete the first full square knot.

19. Repeat steps 17 and 18 down the length of the core cord, leaving about 1″ free at the end. Trim the weaving cords to 1″. Fold the cords to the back, and stitch to hold. Do the same with the core cord at the opposite end of the braid.

20. Repeat to complete the second handle.

Step 19

Complete

21. Attach a decorative bead so that it dangles from the bottom tip of the flower on the purse front. Sew the handles to the insides of the purse front and back, about ½″ inwards from the right and left edges. Add a snap fastener at the center top.

Bugaku Drum

Bugaku is a traditional Japanese musical instrument. Decorative bugaku drums are still played as an accompaniment to dance at Shinto shrines, as well as at the Imperial court. Originating in ancient China and Korea, they are most often heard at New Year, when dances are performed in honor of the gods. Taking its shape from a traditional bugaku drum, this decorative pincushion also doubles as an attractive paperweight or dresser ornament.

Make a flower

1. Follow steps 1 to 6 of *Protea* on pages 17 to 18 to make one flower. Here, the same fabric is used for all eight petals. Note, too, that I did not use a center circle fabric; instead I made sure that a pretty flower motif would show at the center of my folding circle.

Selections

Top and base: **Cotton scraps**

Padding and side panel: **Felt scraps**

Stuffing: **Batting or fabric scraps**

Flower: **Silk or cotton scraps**

Beads: **Four large, eight small**

#25 embroidery floss (6-ply)

See template A on page 137. Use ¼" seam allowance for all sewing, unless directed otherwise.

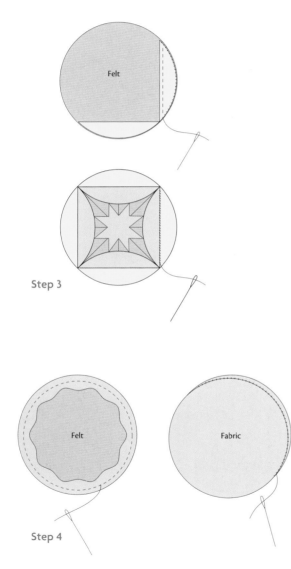

Felt

Step 3

Felt

Fabric

Step 4

Make the drum

2. Make a 3 ⅞ " diameter circle template and cut three from felt. Add ¼" seam allowance to the template (making a 4 ⅜" diameter circle), then cut one from fabric for the base. Cut a strip of felt measuring ¾" × 12 ¼".

3. Using leaf template A, cut four from fabric. Turn the curve under by ⅛", then press to hold. Pin in place onto a felt circle from step 2. Baste along the straight edge, then appliqué around the curve, as shown. Attach the remaining three leaf pieces in the same way. Sew the completed flower from Step 1 to the center of this felt piece, hiding the raw edges of the leaves.

4. Fold in a ¼" seam allowance on the fabric circle from step 1. Press to hold. Slip a felt circle inside the folded-in seam allowance. Sew the felt to the folded-in seam allowance, taking care not to let the needle go through to the fabric front. Sew a second circle of felt to the first, hiding the folded-in seam allowance. Trim the second circle slightly as necessary to complete the base.

5. Pin the felt strip from Step 2 end to end, making a ring. Place the completed base inside the ring. Use embroidery floss and herringbone stitch (see page 13) to attach the ring to the base. When the two ends of the strip meet, use overcast stitch to sew them together. Repeat, this time sewing the remaining long edge of the ring to the top piece. Before closing, stuff firmly with batting or cotton scraps.

6. To embellish, string one large bead and two small beads onto embroidery floss and stitch in place at a corner of the center flower, allowing the beads dangle. Repeat for the other three corners of the flower.

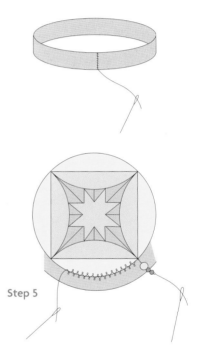

Step 5

Little Drums

小太鼓

Because they are so reminiscent of festivals and holidays, drums are a popular motif in Japanese arts and crafts. Make these little drum trinkets as scissor fobs and give them to friends who sew. Add tiny charms to glasses for a colorful cocktail tray. Anyone can use these little drums as key rings, as party tokens, or for a very special gift wrap. What could be simpler?

Make the drum

1. Cut a 2½" diameter circle of fabric. Position a 1" circle of batting at the center. Gather stitch around the circumference of the fabric, then pull the gathers lightly to form a cup. Insert a button to form the drum base. Add more batting or stuffing, then pull the gathers tight to close the opening and backstitch to hold. Repeat to make a matching drum top.

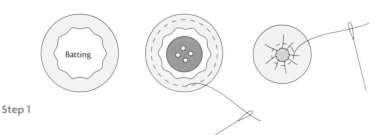

Step 1

Selections

Drum: Scraps

Stuffing: Batting or fabric scraps

2 flat 1" buttons

¼" ribbon: 14"

#25 embroidery floss (6-ply)

Charms or decorative beads

2. Thread and knot a needle with an 18" strand of two-ply embroidery floss. Insert the needle at the same point where the gathers closed. Wrap around the drum base and stitch to secure. Repeat, until the drum base is divided into eight even pie-shaped segments. At the center, where the embroidery threads cross, make a small circle of tiny embroidery stitches. Build outwards, making the circle larger, until the embroidered circle at the center is about ¼" diameter. Repeat this step to make a matching drum top.

3. Hold the drum base and top back to back and, using embroidery floss and herringbone stitch (see page 13), sew the pieces together around the perimeter, leaving about 1" open. Stuff firmly with batting or cotton scraps, then stitch the opening closed.

Step 2

Step 3

Add the ribbon and charm

4. Pin the ribbon tip to the stuffed waistband of the drum. Using a small overcast stitch and starting at the pin, sew one long edge of ribbon halfway around the perimeter, butting up against one of the buttons. Be sure to stop when you reach halfway. Repeat, sewing the other long edge of the same length of ribbon so that it butts up against the second button. Slightly overlap the loose ribbon tip over the sewn tip and stitch it in place. Wrap then sew the long edge around the other half of the top and bottom buttons as before. When complete, a perfect 6" loop of ribbon forms. Stitch a charm or decorative bead to the drum, opposite the loop.

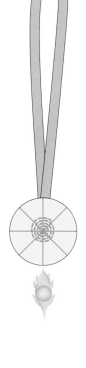

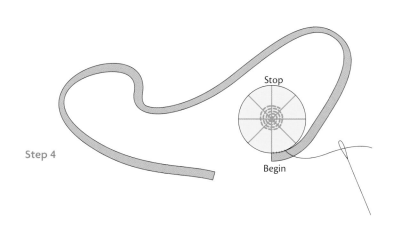

Step 4

Stop

Begin

Hana-no-en

I named this necklace after Hana-no-en, a joyful event in which Japanese people gather to admire the beauty of flowers. I styled the flowers to resemble the Japanese bellflower, a popular motif in wagashi sweets—and my autumn favorite. When creating the necklace, I imagined courtiers and ladies of the Heian era (794-1192) conversing or exchanging poems in a beautiful autumnal garden. The colors I chose for the braiding are inspired by courtly dress and accessories.

Take your time to choose decorative beads to set off your necklace. With a little searching, you can find beautiful lampwork beads like the ones shown here, which complement the necklace design perfectly.

Selections

Flowers and buds: **Cotton scraps**

Padding and backing: **Felt scraps**

Beads: 18 small beads (9 in each of 2 colors); 60 delicas; 3 large decorative beads to dangle; 1 large bead for fastener

#25 embroidery floss (6-ply): Selection of five colors

See template A on page 137. Use ¼" seam allowance for all sewing, unless indicated otherwise.

Make three flowers

1. Make a 3½" diameter circle template, then cut five from fabric. Set two aside. On the remaining three, fold in the raw edge by about ⅛" and press to hold. Make a 1½" diameter circle template, then cut three from felt.

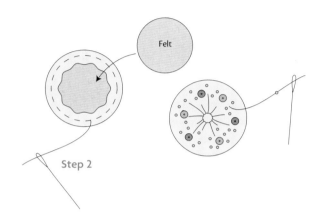

Step 2

2. Pin a felt piece to the wrong side of each of the three fabric pieces. Gather stitch around the circumference of each fabric piece, stitching through the folded-in seam allowance. Pull the gathers tight, completely hiding the felt circles, and backstitch to hold. Remove the pin and press lightly. Sew six small beads and 20 delicas onto each flower as desired.

Make two buds

3. Fold each of the two remaining circles from step 1 in half, right side out. Fold inwards along the fold-lines shown. Fold the top layer back again, by about ³/₈", to give the bud more dimension. Gather stitch around the curve through all layers. Pull the gathers gently to create a petal shape, then backstitch to hold.

Step 3

Weave two braids

4. For each braid, cut five 30" strands of 6-ply embroidery floss, selecting colors to create a rainbow effect. I chose blue (A), green (B), pink (C), magenta (D), and purple (E).

5. Make a knot at one end to tie all five colored strands together. Pin the knot to a sturdy pincushion or corkboard.

6. Pick up strand A (the working strand) in your left hand and strand B in your right. Working left to right, make a half-knot by weaving A *over* then back *under* B and up through the loop. Make sure you hold B taut, while pulling on A to tighten the knot. Repeat to complete a full knot. Drop B and pick up C. Still using A as the working strand, make another full knot (two half knots). Continue through D and E, still using A as the working strand.

7. Repeat step 6, using B as the working strand and weaving through C, D, E, and A in sequence.

8. Repeat step 6, using C as the working strand and weaving through D, E, A, and B.

9. Repeat step 6, using D as the working strand and weaving through E, A, B, and C.

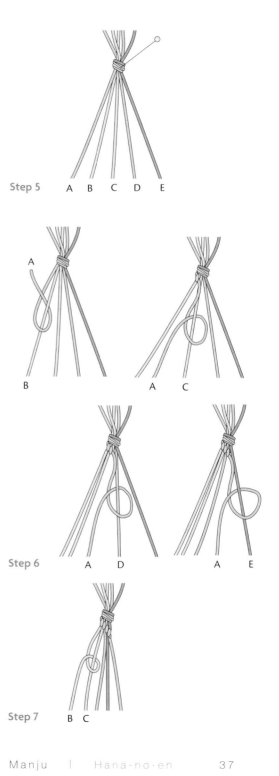

Step 5   A   B   C   D   E

Step 6   A   D   A   E

Step 7   B   C

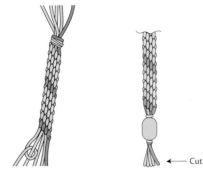

Step 10

← Cut

Step 11

10. Repeat steps 6 through 9 until the braid measures 6".

11. Gather the ends of the strands together and string them through a large decorative bead. Tie a knot to hold the bead in place. If necessary, trim the strands to about ½".

12 Repeat steps 5 to 10 to make a second braid. In the last row, weave knots over just two strands (not the usual four). Hold the working strand in your right hand and separate the other strands into sets of two. Put the working strand aside for now. Knot the ends of the two sets together to form a ½" loop (or the correct size to fit your bead from step 11). Trim the threads close to the knot.

13. Pick up the working strand and wrap it around the loop, knotting as you go. Work your way around the entire loop. Knot off and trim.

¾"

← Trim

Step 12

A

Step 13

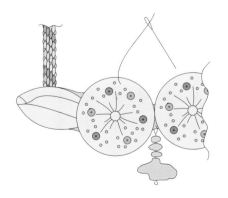

Complete

14. With template A, cut two from felt. Pin the ends of the braids in place, about ½" inwards from either end and sandwiched between the two felt pieces. Use overcast stitch to sew the felt pieces together around the entire perimeter, trapping the ends of the braids between them. Remove the pins. Position then sew the buds in place on the front. Sew the flowers so that they overlap and hide the previous set of stitches. If desired, add decorative beads or short strings of beads, allowing them to dangle as shown.

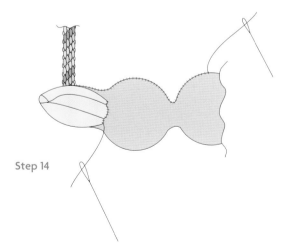

Step 14

Berry, Berry

Little red birds, why are you so red?

We eat red berries.

Little blue birds, why are you so blue?

We eat blue berries.

Little white birds, why are you white?

We eat white berries.

I love the simplicity of the lyrics of this traditional Japanese children's poem. When I was little, I would sing this song as I ran through the fields and hillsides to gather nuts and berries. Today, I still sing it to myself as I walk in my garden. On this pretty cell cozy, beaded yo-yos that remind me of berries sit atop a fabric patterned with flower buds. I used a two-color ombre-dyed fabric for the yo-yos.

Make three yo-yos

1. Make a 2 ½" diameter circle template, then cut three from fabric. Fold in the raw edges by about ¼" and press to hold.

Selections

Cozy fabric: ⅛ yard or less

Lining: ⅛ yard of less

Padding: ⅛ yard or less of felt

Yo-yos: Scraps of cotton or silk

Beads: 15 or 18 small round beads

#25 embroidery floss (6-ply)

2 snap fasteners

See templates A to D on pages 138 to 139. Use ¼" seam allowance for all sewing, unless indicated otherwise.

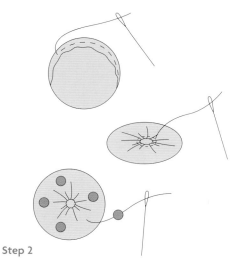

Step 2

Felt

Step 4

Lining

Step 5

2. Gather stitch around the circumference, through the folded-in seam allowance. Pull the gathers tight and backstitch to hold. Press lightly. Sew five or six beads to each yo-yo, as shown in the photograph.

Make the cozy

3. With templates A, B, and C, cut one each from felt. Add ¼" seam allowance to each template, then cut one each from fabric, plus one more each from lining fabric.

4. Fold in a ¼" seam allowances on fabric pieces A, B, and C, and press to hold. Slip a corresponding felt piece inside the folded-in seam allowance of each fabric piece. Sew the felt to the folded-in seam allowance, taking care not to let the needle go through to the fabric front. Stitch the yo-yos in place onto the cozy front.

5. Using lining piece A from Step 2, fold in and press a ¼" seam allowance. Pin the lining piece to the felt side of the cozy front. Working from the lining side, use overcast stitch to sew the piece in place, hiding the felt padding. Repeat with pieces B and C to complete the cozy back and the side panel.

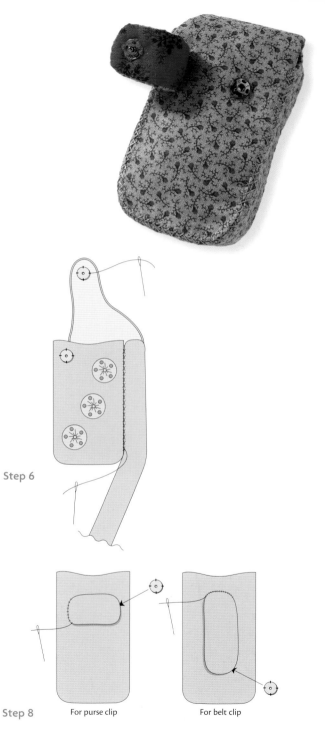

6. Beginning at the top right, position then pin one long edge of the covered strip C in place along the edge of the cozy front. Wrap around the right side, bottom, and left side of the cozy. Using embroidery floss and herringbone stitch (see page 13), worked from the front, sew the strip in place, removing pins as you go. Repeat, this time wrapping the other edge of the strip around the right side, bottom, and left side of the cozy back.

Complete

7. Sew a snap fastener to the top left the cozy front and to the inside top of the cozy back.

Optional belt or purse clip

8. With template D, cut one from felt. Add ¼" seam allowance to the template, then cut one each from fabric and lining fabric. Follow steps 4 and 5 above to complete the belt clip. Sew along one short edge to the back of the cozy as shown, then add a snap fastener at the other end to close.

Step 6

Step 8   For purse clip   For belt clip

Higashi

Bittersweet and impossibly delicate, *higashi* are those tiny, intricately designed dry candies most often seen at a traditional Japanese Tea Ceremony, where they are admired as an integral part of the artistic setting. I am often astounded by the fine workmanship of the candy artisans who make *higashi*, and I strive to make my creations in fabrics as perfect as the ones they craft from rice flour and sugar.

平菓子

Hana-Chiru-Sato

This elegant dianthus flower was inspired by a beautiful box of wagashi candy given to me by a friend of my aunt who visited from Kyoto. The box was crafted from lightweight paulonia wood, and upon opening the lid I saw delicately arranged rows of sweet rice-flour candies, shaped into autumn flowers—bellflowers, daisies, and dianthus. They were so pretty I could not bear even to taste one. Instead, I kept them among my special treasures. A memory of those wagashi flowers led me to create this necklace. I imagine the flowers gently swinging in the autumn wind along a quiet country pathway. Notice that the braid design is quite challenging; you may want to make Protea on page 18 before attempting this complex but beautiful pattern.

Make two flowers

1. Using pentagon template A on page 140, cut four pentagons (two each from two complimentary fabrics). Match the pieces into contrasting pairs. Follow the directions on page 8 to prepare the pentagons for folding.

Selections

Flowers: Scraps of two different fabrics

Backing: Scrap of felt

Beads: 60 delica beads

Decorative cord: About 3 yards in each of 3 colors

See templates A and B on page 140. Use ¼" seam allowance for sewing, unless otherwise indicated.

2. With the inside fabric facing, mark dots at 1/4" inwards from each angle. Mark dots at $5/8$" inwards from the midpoint of each pentagon side. Draw lines to connect the dots, creating a star shape at the center of the pentagon. With the diagram as a guide, fold line 1 to line 1 and use a running stitch to sew though all layers. In the same way, fold line 2 to line 2, 3 to 3, 4 to 4, and 5 to 5, stitching the sides of the star together.

3. "Flatten" the flower, by pushing up from the base so that a pentagon shape is recreated and the inner tips of all five petals are at the center top (A). If necessary, add a stitch or two at A to make sure the inner tips are snug against each other. Fold back each side of each petal, wrapping the outer tip to the back. Use an awl or a chopstick to make each fold neat, precisely creating the flower shape.

4. Sew six beads to the petals of each flower.

Step 2

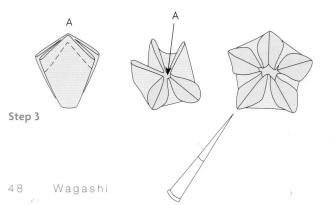

Step 3

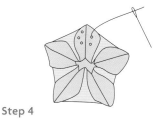

Step 4

Weave two braids

5. Cut two lengths each of cord measuring 40″ (A, shown in blue), 55″ (B, green), and 62″ (C, purple). Fold each in half, marking the midpoints with pins. Pin each to a firm pincushion or corkboard, butting the cords up next to each other and making sure B is at the center, C is at the top, and A is at the bottom, as shown.

6. Begin by working with the right-side A, B, C cords only. Hold blue cord A (which acts as a core cord) in your left hand. Pick up purple C and weave it *under* A, then wrap upwards around A and downward through the loop as shown. Pull both cords gently to tighten this half-hitch knot, making sure it butts up tightly against the pins. Repeat to make a second purple half-hitch knot. Lay the right-side cords aside for now.

7. Moving to the left-side cords, repeat step 6. This time you will hold blue cord A in your right hand, and purple cord C in your left. The resulting purple knots will mirror-image the knots on the right. Make sure the knots butt up tightly against the pins to form a continuous pattern.

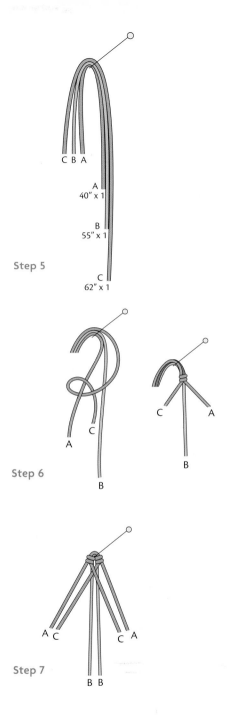

Step 5

A
40″ x 1

B
55″ x 1

C
62″ x 1

Step 6

Step 7

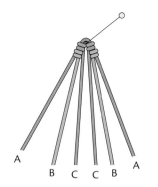

Step 9

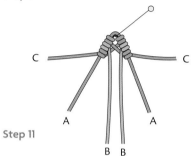

Step 11

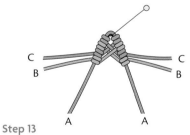

Step 13

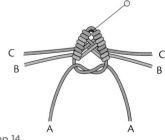

Step 14

8. Switch back to the right side. Hold blue cord A in your right hand. This time, pick up green cord B and weave it *under* A, then wrap upwards around A and downward through the loop. As before, pull both cords gently to tighten the knot, butting it up against the previous row. Repeat to make a second green half-hitch knot.

9. Moving to the left-side cords, repeat step 8. This time you will hold blue cord A in your left hand and green cord B in your right. You will make two green half-hitch knots that mirror-image the right-side pair.

10. With your left hand, pick up the left-side purple C cord. Weave it *under* the other C cord, *over* the right-side green B cord, and *under* the right-side blue A cord. Using this purple C cord and the right-side blue A cord, make two more purple half-hitch knots as in step 6.

11. With your right hand, pick up the other purple C cord. Weave it *under* the left-side green B and blue A cords. Make two more purple half-hitch knots as in step 7.

12. With your left hand, pick up the left-side green B cord. Weave it *under* the right-side green B and blue A cords. Make two more green half-hitch knots as in step 8.

13. With your right hand, pick up the other green C cord. Weave it *under* the left-side blue A cord. Make two more green half-hitch knots as in step 9.

14. Make a simple overhand knot using the blue A cords. This will pull the half-hitch stitches into a symmetrical rounded diamond shape. Manipulate the knotted A cords so that one lies neatly on top of the other.

15. Repeat steps 6 to 14 to complete five more rounded diamond shapes.

16. With your left hand, pick up the right-side green B cord. Weave it *under* the right-side purple C cord. Make two green half-hitch knots. (Notice you are now using the purple C cord as the core cord, not the blue A cord as before.) Repeat on the left side, making two mirror-image green knots.

17. Repeat step 16, this time using the blue A cord to make pairs of blue half-hitch knots. Finish this row with an overhand knot (see step 14) using the purple C cords.

18. With your left hand, pick up the right-side blue A cord. Weave it *under* the right-side green B cord. Make two blue half-hitch knots. (Notice you are now using the green B cord as the core cord). Repeat on the left side, making two mirror-image blue knots.

Step 15

Step 17

Step 19

Step 22

Step 23

19. Repeat step 18, this time using the purple C cord to make pairs of purple half-hitch knots. Finish this row with an overhand knot (see step 14) using the green B cords. Draw the blue A cord to the back of the work, pull gently to make sure the weaves are tight, then trim to about 1". Sew the end of the cord to the back of the work to secure.

20. With your left hand, pick up the right-side green B cord. Weave it *under* the right-side purple C cord. Make two green half-hitch knots. Repeat on the left side, making two mirror-image green knots. Finish this row with an overhand knot (see step 14) using the purple C cords.

21. With your left hand, pick up the right-side purple C cord. Weave it *under* the right-side green B cord. Make two purple half-hitch knots. Repeat on the left side, making two mirror-image purple knots. Finish this row with an overhand knot (see step 14) using the green B cords.

22. Repeat step 21 to make another pair of purple half-hitch knots on either side. Draw the green B cord to the back of the work, pull gently to make sure the weaves are tight, then trim to about 1". Sew the end of the cord to the back of the work to secure. Finish this row with an overhand knot (see step 14) using the purple C cords.

23. Take both loose cords in one hand and make a double overhand knot as shown at the ends. Trim off any excess cord close to the knot.
24. Make the second braid in the same way.

Complete

25. Using template B on page 140, cut two from felt. Position the first square knot of each finished braid so that it overlaps onto a felt piece as shown. Overstitch in place.
26. Position the flowers prettily on top of the felt base, overlapping them very slightly. Secure each flower with a few stitches through the felt layer. Hem-stitch the second felt piece over the first, trapping the ends of the braids firmly and neatly inside.

Step 25

3/4"

Dandelion

When we were young, my sister would bake a sponge cake for me every Sunday afternoon. Sometimes, she would finish it off by sprinkling silver sparkles over the cream, reminding me of stars falling from the sky. Other times, she would put grated lemon rinds in the dough and make pretty yellow doughnut rings. The colors I chose for Dandelion *remind me of those long-ago Sundays.*

Make three yo-yos

1. Make a 5 ½" diameter circle template, then cut three from fabric. Fold in the raw edges by ¼" and press to hold. Gather stitch around the circumference, through the folded-in seam. Pull the gathers tight and backstitch to hold. Press lightly. Sew 11 delica beads to each yo-yo, as shown in the photograph.

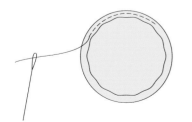 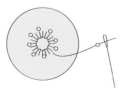

Step 1

Selections

Purse fabric: ⅛ yard or less of cotton or silk

Lining: ⅛ yard of less of cotton or silk

Padding: ⅛ yard or less of felt

Leaves and stems: Scraps of green patterned fabrics

Yo-yos: Scraps of cotton or silk

Beads: 33 small round beads; 11 mid-size beads; large decorative bead

Decorative cord or craft cord: About 2 ¾ yards

#25 embroidery floss (6-ply)

See templates A, B, and C on pages 141 to 142. Use ½" seam allowance for purse pieces only; use ¼" seam allowance for other sewing.

Back view

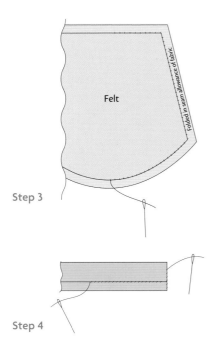

Felt

Folded in seam allowance of fabric

Step 3

Step 4

Make the purse

2. With template A, cut two from felt. Add ½" seam allowance to the template, then cut two from fabric for the front and back, plus two from lining fabric. Cut a strip of felt measuring ⅝" x 22", plus two strips of fabric measuring 1½" x 23".

3. Fold in the seam allowances on fabric pieces A and press to hold. Slip a corresponding felt piece inside the folded-in seam allowances. Sew the felt to the folded-in seam allowance, taking care not to let needle go through to the fabric front.

4. Press a ¼" seam allowance around all edges of the fabric strip from step 2. Completely wrap the felt strip inside, then use overcast stitch to encase it. Press the covered strip.

5. Cut two from fabric using leaf template B (reversing the template for the second piece); cut one from fabric using leaf template C. Turn in the seam allowances and press. Wrap the wide section of the seam (as shown on each template) around the edge of the purse front, and pin in place. Appliqué the leaves onto the purse front. Cut four strips of fabric on the bias, each ½″ x 6″. Turn under a narrow ⅛″ seam allowance and press. Position the strips on the purse front, curving to resemble stems, as in the photograph. Pin then appliqué in place. Embellish the purse front with beads, as desired.

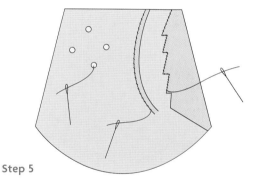

Step 5

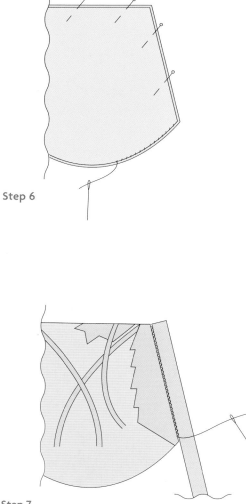

Step 6

Step 7

6. Using the lining pieces A from Step 2, turn under and press a ½" seam allowance. Pin the lining pieces to the felt sides of the purse front and back, trapping the turned-under seams of the leaf templates from step 5 in place. Working from the lining side, use overstitch to sew each piece in place, hiding the felt padding and the raw edges of the leaves.

7. Beginning at the top right, position then pin one long edge of the covered strip from step 4 in place along the edge of the pouch front. Wrap around the right side, bottom, and left side of the purse. Using a 2-ply strand of embroidery floss and herringbone stitch, worked from the pouch front, sew the strip in place, removing the pins as you go (see page13). Repeat, this time wrapping the other edge of the strip around the right side, bottom, and left side of the pouch back.

Weave a square-knot handle

8. Cut a length of cord measuring 13" (core cord) and another measuring 104" (weaving cord). Follow steps 15 to 19 of *Protea* on pages 24 to 25 to complete a 13" handle.

Complete

9. Make a button loop at the top center of the outside back of the purse. Begin by knotting two 8" strands of 6-ply embroidery floss together. Thread both strands through the same needle. Draw the needle from the inside back lining to the outside back, allowing the knot to sit tight against the inside back lining. Pin the knot to secure in place.

10. Make a series of half-knots as shown, until the knotted strand measures about 3". For each half-knot, hold strand B firmly in your left hand. Weave strand A *over* then *under* B, then up through the loop. Pull on both strands to tighten the half-knot. Rethread both strands though the needle, then draw them back through to the inside back of the purse, forming a button loop. Knot the ends and trim any loose ends of embroidery floss.

11. Sew the yo-yos to the front of the purse, hiding the tips of the stems, using the photograph as a guide. Sew a decorative bead or button at the top center of the purse front. Sew the handle to the outside of the side panels, overlapping about 1½" at the top.

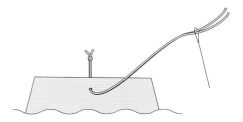

Step 9

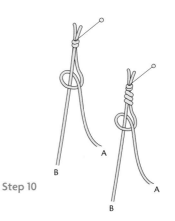

Step 10

Step 11

Wagashi

The elaborately designed candies that are a focus of the traditional Japanese tea ceremony have their origins in the ancient city of Kyoto in western Japan. During the ancient Heian period (794 to 1192 AD), Kyoto was the capital city and the center of Japan's aristocratic court. Here, a luxuriant culture came into full bloom as Kyoto entered a golden age of art and literature. Buddhist sculpture, yamato-e painting, and the silk weaving tradition all have their roots in Kyoto. While this gracious city long ceased to function as the Imperial capital, it will always be the artistic heart of Japan.

The growing popularity of the tea ceremony during the Edo period (1603 to 1867) persuaded Kyoto artisans to turn their attention to candies. Served to offset the bitterness of the tea, *wagashi* have an important aesthetic purpose, too. Shaped and colored to remind us of seasonal flowers or fruits, *wagashi* help guests enter the spirit of the tea ceremony. In time-honored tradition, each guest praises such elements of the ceremony as the tea bowls, the setting, and, naturally, the *wagashi*. The selected designs might carry special meaning, which the host then shares. Of course, not all Japanese sweets are of the beautiful, delicate kind we associate with the tea ceremony. As you read, you will find out about other delicious varieties.

The Humble Azuki Bean

Of course, the appeal of candies reaches far beyond ceremonial protocol. Traditional Japanese sweets are made by cooking red or white azuki beans with sugar until they form a paste. Soft and pliable, the paste molds easily into a variety of shapes. This is done by skilled confectioners, in much the same way that French or Swiss pastry cooks work with marzipan. With the natural world as inspiration, beautiful fruits and flowers, tiny animals, and crescent moons are all pretty and popular motifs.

Wagashi come in a variety of shapes, tastes, textures, and sizes. Some of my favorites are steamed

Artistry

rice dumplings with a small ball of sweet bean paste inside. The sweet is usually folded between camellia leaves or wrapped in salted cherry leaves. Sometimes, the dumplings are wrapped in large bamboo leaves, then steamed again. The leaves impart delicate seasonal aromas to the dumplings.

Wagashi Memories

I have warm memories of *wagashi*, particularly during the period of my childhood when I lived with my aunt in Kamakura, another Japanese city that is rich in cultural traditions. My aunt lived on the grounds of a shrine and she would always keep small boxes of a special chrysanthemum-shaped cake, *okumotsu* stacked near the alter. As visitors left the shrine, she would hand them a box of these pink and white delights as a parting gift. While I loved to see the pretty shapes of the candies inside, I looked forward most to the delicious taste of sweet bean paste when I bit into the cakes.

My aunt ordered her *wagashi* from a local confectioner, who would send her a catalog from which to make her selections. Each month, the shop would offer beautiful candies molded into a different flower design. One spring morning, our box arrived with a fresh branch of plum blossoms on top. Such elegance! We could not but admire the thoughtfulness of the shop owner who so clearly valued traditional Japanese aesthetics. Like many sweet shops in Japan, our local confectionary was very low key. There was not so much as a sign on the door, yet everyone knew of the treasures within. To reach the shop, we would walk through a narrow passage, lined with tall bamboo trees. The trees would rustle gently to announce our arrival. At the end of the path was an elegant lattice gate, with the name of the shop gently brushed in Japanese calligraphy. There were no candy displays or window dressing or even a sign to announce that this was a sweet shop. This subtlety added to the pleasure of our visit.

Braided Delights

As I worked on these projects, I imagined all kinds of pretty wagashi: *Cherries on top of a cake, cherry blossom petals suspended in jelly, a pale blue morning glory made of sugar sitting on top of a chilled summer dessert. I fashioned my bookmarks by recreating those images in embroidery threads and fabric. What fun to find one of these in a new book! While the instructions here specify easy-to-find embroidery floss, you can experiment with different types of thread, ribbon, cord, or macramé string to give your braids an entirely different look and texture. I enjoy working with delicate Japanese cords; you will soon find your favorite braiding materials.*

Weave a 9" braid

1. Cut two strands in each of four colors of 6-ply embroidery floss, each measuring 76". (In the drawings, A is green, B is red, C is purple, and D is yellow.) Group each color together (making a 12-ply strand), then fold each in half and pin at the midpoints to a firm pincushion.

Selections

Flowers, berries, and leaves: **Cotton scraps**

Leaves: **Felt scraps**

Braids: **#25 embroidery floss (6-ply) in four colors**

See templates A to D on page 142

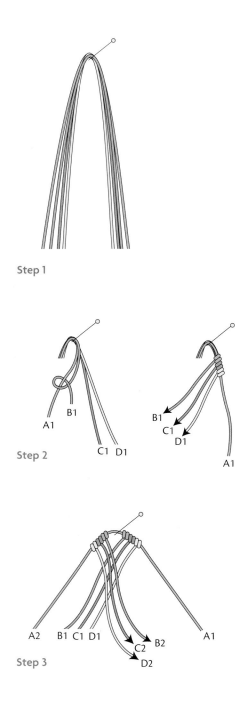

Step 1

Step 2

Step 3

2. Begin by working with the right-side A1, B1, C1, and D1 strands only. Hold green strand A1 (which acts as a core strand) in your left hand. Pick up red B1 and weave it *over* A1, then wrap upwards around A1 and downward through the loop as shown. Pull both cords gently to tighten this half-hitch knot, making sure it butts up tightly against the pins. Repeat to make a second red half-hitch knot. Put down the red and pick up the purple C1. Make two purple half-hitch knots. Next, pick up yellow D1 and make two yellow half-hitch knots. Lay the right-hand strands aside for now.

3. Moving to the left-side strands A2, B2, C2, and D2, repeat step 2. As before, you will be wrapping each color in turn around green strand A2. The resulting red, purple, and yellow knots will mirror-image the knots on the right. Make sure the knots butt up tightly against each other to form a continuous pattern.

4. With your right hand, pick up the red B1 strand. Weave it *over* the red B2 strand, *under* the purple C2 strand, and *over* the yellow D2 strand. Pick up the green A2 strand in your left hand and make two red half-hitch knots around it as in step 2.

5. With your right hand, pick up the purple C1 strand. Weave it *under* the red B2 strand, *over* the purple C2 strand, and *under* the yellow D2 strand. Pick up the green A2 strand in your left hand and make two purple half-hitch knots around it as in step 2.

6. With your right hand, pick up the yellow D1 strand. Weave it *over* the red B2 strand, *under* the purple C2 strand, and *over* the yellow D2 strand.

7. Pick up the green A2 strand in your left hand and make two yellow half-hitch knots around it as in step 2. Notice the pretty weaving pattern you are creating at the center as the knots form.

8. Working with strands A1, B2, C2, and D2, make two red, purple, and yellow half-hitch knots around green A1, as before.

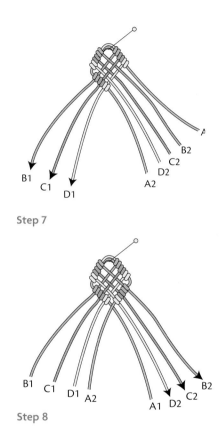

Step 7

Step 8

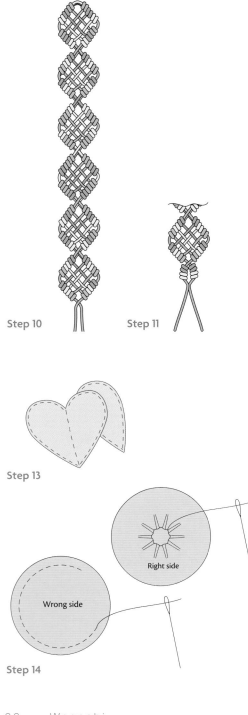

Step 10

Step 11

Step 13

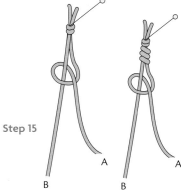

Right side

Wrong side

Step 14

9. Make a simple overhand knot using the green A cords. (See step 14 of *Hana-Chiru-Sato* on page 49). This will pull the half-hitch stitches into a symmetrical rounded diamond shape. Manipulate the knotted A cords so that they lie side by side at the bottom of the diamond. You will now have a complete diamond, with weaving at the center.

10. Repeat steps 2 to 9 to complete several more rounded diamond shapes. With each new diamond, switch to a new color for the core cord, working through the colors in sequence. Continue until your braid measure 9" or the desired length.

11. To finish the braid, repeat steps 7 to 9 three times, creating three mirror-image rows of half-hitch knots below the last diamond. You may alternate colors as you please. Make an overhand knot at the end of each row.

12. Trim all but two same-color strands to about ½" and sew them neatly to the back of the braid.

Step 15

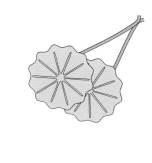

A

B

A

B

Complete Design A

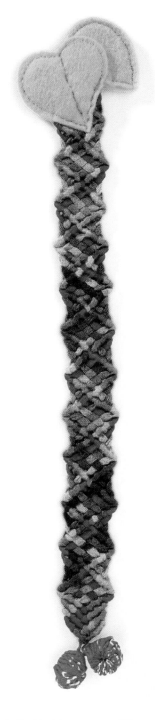

13. Cut 2 from felt, using templates A and B. Sew around the stitch lines shown in the drawing, sewing the pieces together. Pin one end of the braid between the felt A pieces. Pin the completed B piece between A as shown. Sew along the stitch lines shown on B, sandwiching the top of the braid and B between the two felt A pieces.

14. For the yo-yos, cut two 3" diameter circles of fabric. Fold in a ⅛" seam allowance. Gather stitch around the circumference. Pull gathers tight, stuffing with scraps of batting, if desired. Backstitch to hold. Make two.

15. Thread a needle with two strands of same-color embroidery thread and make a stitch to secure to the center of the first yo-yo. Make a series of half-knots as shown, until the knotted strand measures about ½". For each half-knot, hold strand B firmly in your left hand. Weave strand A *over* then *under* B, then up through the loop. Pull on both strands to tighten the half-knot. Rethread both strands though the needle, then draw them through the bottom tip of the braid, stitching to secure. Make a second series of half knots for another ½". Rethread the needle, then secure to the second yo-yo. Both yo-yos will now dangle from the bottom of the braid.

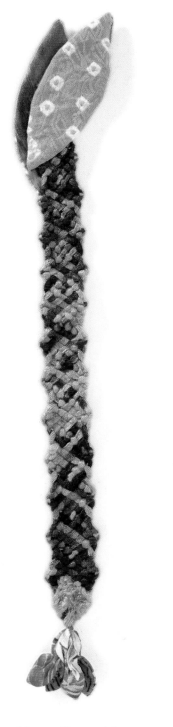

Complete Design B

16. Using template C, cut two each from two different fabrics. Right sides together, sew around the circumference, leaving about 1" open. Turn right side out and press, then blindstitch the opening closed. Overlap the leaves as shown in the photograph, then pin the top of the braid between them. Sew through all layers, trapping the braid between the leaves.

17. Cut two 2" squares from two complementary fabrics. Rights sides together and using a $\frac{1}{8}$" seam allowance, sew around the perimeter, leaving about 1" open. Turn right side out and press, then blindstitch the opening closed. Gather stitch as shown, through both layers. Pull the gathers tight and backstitch to hold. Make one or two stitches to secure the flower to the bottom tip of the braid.

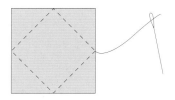

Step 17

Complete Design C

18. Cut two from felt, using template D. Sandwich the top of the braid between the felt pieces, as in the photograph, and pin to hold. Sew around the perimeter, about ⅛" inwards from the edge, sewing the pieces together and trapping the braid inside.

19. Cut two 3" diameter circles from complementary fabrics. Rights sides together and using a ⅛" seam allowance, sew around the circumference, leaving about 1" open. Turn right side out and press, then blindstitch the opening closed. Fold then gather-stitch a shown, sewing through all layers. Pull the gathers tight and backstitch to hold. Sew to flower to the bottom tip of the braid, as in the photograph.

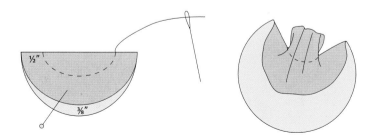

Step 19

Camellia Cache

To make the flower displayed in this project, I recycled a silk dress that I dearly loved. I had not worn this dress for many years, but I did not have the heart to throw it away and kept it in my chest of drawers. Finally, I allowed the dress to live again as a camellia blossom. I especially like the swirls in the pattern that make the flower so vivid. For the leaves, I used a haori *day jacket that had belonged to my mother. The checkered pattern gives the cache its art deco style.*

Begin the cache

1. Make a circle template measuring 4" in diameter. Cut two from felt. Add ¼" seam allowance to the template for a 4½" diameter circle, then cut one from fabric for the back of the cache, plus two more from lining fabric. Cut two strips of fabric on the bias, measuring 1¼" x 13½".

Selections

Cache, leaves, and handle: Silk or cotton scraps

Padding: Felt scraps

Stuffing: Batting scraps

Flower: Silk or cotton scraps

See template A on page 143. Use ¼" seam allowance for all sewing.

Back view

Felt

Step 2

2. Fold in a ¼" seam allowance on the fabric circle for the back of the cache and on both circles of lining fabric, then press to hold. Slip a felt circle inside the folded-in seam allowance of each of the lining circles. Sew the felt to the folded-in seam allowance, taking care not to let needle go through to the lining front. Set one aside. Slip the other inside the folded-in seam allowance of the fabric circle. Sew through the folded-in seam allowance, again taking care not to let the needle go through to the fabric front. This is the back of the cache.

3. For the piping, fold one of the bias strips from step 1 in half lengthwise, then press under a ¼" seam allowance around all sides. Pin one long edge to the back of the cache, and use a small overcast stitch to sew it in place around the entire circumference. Wrap the other long edge to the lining side, then stitch it in place as before.

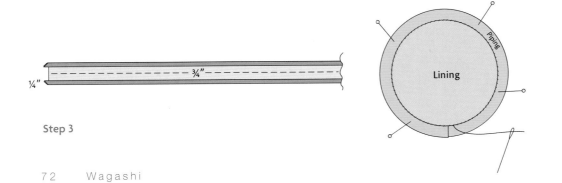

¾"

¼"

Step 3

piping

Lining

Make a flower

4. Cut the following square/rectangles of fabric:

   1" × 1": Cut 1
   1" × 1½": Cut 6
   2" × 2½": Cut 3
   2" × 4": Cut 3
   2" × 5": Cut 3

5. Pin the 1" x 1" square to the center of the felt side of the remaining felt-backed circle from step 2. Baste it in place.

6. Fold three 1" × 1½" rectangles in half lengthwise, inserting a thin layer of batting inside. Position as shown, with the folded edge toward the center of the felt circle. Pin, then baste each folded rectangle in place, overlapping as shown and stitching along the long outer edge.

7. Repeat with the remaining three 1" × 1½" rectangles, lining each with a thin layer of batting and overlapping as shown. Repeat, this time using the 2" × 2½" rectangles.

8. Fold, stuff, and position the 2" × 4" rectangles as before. This time, manipulate the outer edge into a curve before stitching in place, as shown.

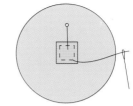

Step 5

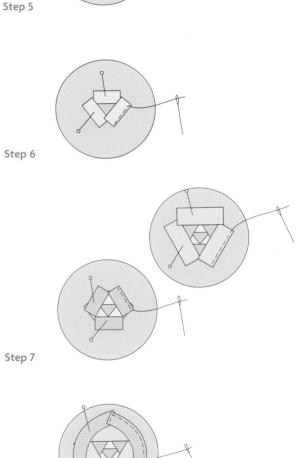

Step 6

Step 7

Step 8

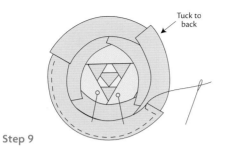

Step 9

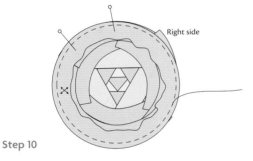

Step 10

9. Fold, stuff, and position the 2" × 5" rectangles, curving as before and tucking the outer edge to the back of the felt circle before basting in place. This is the cache front.

10. Turn under a ¼" seam allowance along all edges of the remaining bias strip from Step 1. Right sides together and aligning the edges, pin the strip around the circumference of the cache front. Sew in place around the entire perimeter. Appliqué the remaining long edge in place to the other side of the cache front.

Complete

11. Using leaf template A, cut two each from two different fabrics. Matching contrasting fabrics and right sides together, sew around the perimeter, leaving 1" open. Turn right side out, and blindstitch the opening closed. Press.

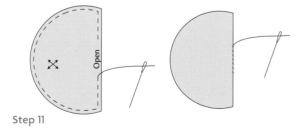

Step 11

12. Gather stitch along the long edge. Fold the leaf in half, then pull the thread lightly to gather. Backstitch to hold. Sew one leaf to the outside back of the cache, allowing it to overlap the edge, so that it is visible from the front, as shown in the photograph.

13. Cut a strip of fabric measuring 1" × 7½". Fold in half then sew along the long edges to make a tube. Turn right side out and press. Turn the ends to the inside of the tube, hiding the raw edges. Fold the handle in half, then sew the ends to the inside of the cache front. Sew the remaining leaf to back of the handle tube, so that it is completely visible from the front of the cache.

14. Use a running stitch through all layers to sew the front to the back. Stitch around the circumference, leaving about 4" around the curve open at the top.

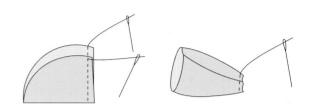

Step 12

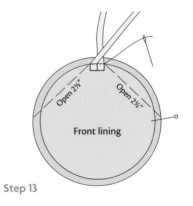

Open 2½" Open 2½"

Front lining

Step 13

Namagashi

Rice, the staple of Japanese cuisine, is a key

ingredient of *wagashi*, too. Japanese rice cakes,

or *namagashi*, are a favorite accompaniment to

green tea, offsetting its slightly bitter taste with a little

something sweet. Rice cakes are easily kneaded

into a dough that can be shaped into lovely mounds,

pretty flowers, butterflies, or seasonal fruits. I hope

you find the projects in this chapter to be as sweet

and light hearted as the most flavorsome *namagashi*.

Purple Dianthus

I have a clear memory of seeing a purple dianthus flower during my high school years. I had stayed over at a friend's house. It was a stormy night, but we awoke to a brilliantly blue sky, and a neighbor invited us to go for a drive. It was approaching the end of autumn, and the hills were covered with Japanese grasses swaying in the breeze. Among the thick silver grasses, I saw a dash of bright purple. No one but me noticed the flower.

Shown here as a decorative belt, this project is shown as a necklace on the next page. If you wish to make it as a belt, simply lengthen the braid as desired. For this necklace, I teamed silk kimono fabric with cotton. The wooden buttons on either side are from my collection, but you will enjoy finding some that work equally well at your favorite bead store.

Make a flower

1. Using template A from *Hana-Chiru-Sato* on page 140, cut two pentagons, each from a different fabric. Follow the directions on page 8 to prepare the pentagons for folding.

Selections

Necklace front: **Cotton scraps in rich florals**

Padding and backing: **Felt scraps**

Beads: **2 large wooden or decorative buttons (with 2 large holes); 1 large decorative bead; 15 delica beads; 15 small bugle beads**

Cord: **4 ¼ yards**

See template A from Hana-Chiru-Sato on page 140, and templates B and C on page 143. Use ¼" seam allowance unless otherwise indicated.

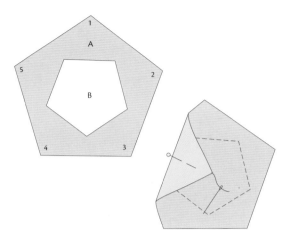

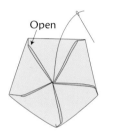

Open

3/4"

A B

Step 2

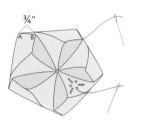

Felt

Step 4

2. Cut template B from card and position this small pentagon upside down on the sewn A pentagons as shown. Mark around the perimeter then set B aside. Fold one point of fabric pentagon A inwards toward the center and stitch to hold. Pin then press the fold firmly. Working clockwise around the pentagon, fold, stitch at the center, then press each fold firmly. You will need to tuck the last fold under the first to complete a perfect small pentagon. Open each side at point A to reveal the inside fabric. Press the folded side firmly. Pin, then stitch at the tip at point B, as shown. In each open area, sew three bugle beads and three delica beads in place into a flower pattern as shown. Sew a large decorative bead to the flower center.

Make the necklace

3. With template C, cut 4 from felt. Add ½" seam allowance to the template, then cut two from fabric, reversing the template for the second piece.

4. Fold in a ½" seam allowance on fabric pieces C, then press to hold. Slip a corresponding felt piece inside the folded-in seam allowance of each fabric piece. Sew the felt to the folded-in seam allowance, taking care not to let needle go through to the fabric front. Sew a second felt piece to the first, hiding the folded-in seam allow-

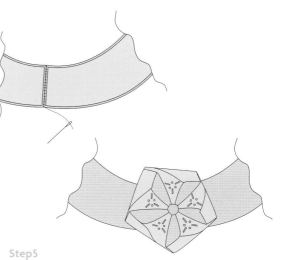

ance. Trim the felt piece slightly as necessary, so that no felt shows when viewed from the fabric side.

5. Working from the back, sew the left and right sides of the necklace together down the center. At the front, sew the flower over the center seam.

Weave two braids

6. For each braid, cut two 37" lengths of cord (total of four). Fold each in half, marking the midpoints.

7. For the first braid, fold a cord over at its midpoint and thread the folded end through one of the holes in the button, making a loop. Thread the loose ends through the loop, from front to back. Pull tight. Repeat, wrapping the second cord around the second hole. Before beginning braiding, tape the button to a hard surface, for extra stability.

Step5

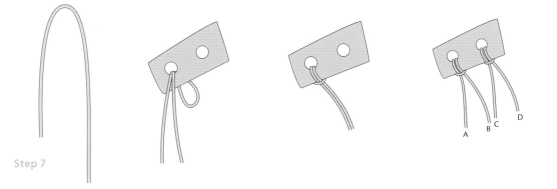

Step 7

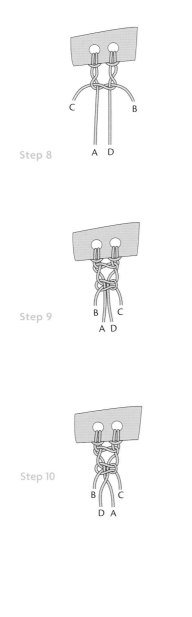

Step 8

Step 9

Step 10

8. Form a half-knot using strands B and C by wrapping strand C *under* strand B. Hold in place with your thumb. Wrap strand B around and *under* strand C, then up through the loop. Weave strand A *under* the top portion of strand B, then down through the loop, moving *under* strand C while moving *over* strand B as shown. Pick up strand D and weave it *under* the top portion of strand C, then down through the loop, moving *over* strand B while moving *under* strand C, as shown.

9. Pick up strand B, wrap it *under* strands A and D. Hold in place with your thumb. Pick up strand C, wrap it *under* strand B, then *over* strands A and D, and *down* through the loop created by strand B, as shown.

10. Cross strand D over strand A, then move strand D to the far left side, *over* strand B. Move strand A to the far right side, *over* strand C.

11. Leave a small amount of space, then form the next half-knot using strands A and D by wrapping strand A *under* strand D. Hold in place with your thumb. Wrap strand D around and *under* strand A, then up through the loop. Weave strand B *under* the top portion of strand D, then down through the loop, moving *under* strand A, while moving *over* strand D. Pick up strand C and weave it *under* the top portion of strand A, then down through the loop. moving *over* strand D while moving *under* strand A.

12. Pick up strand D, wrap it *under* strands B and C. Hold in place with your thumb. Pick up strand A, wrap it *under* strand D, then *over* strands B and C, and *down* through the loop created by strand D as shown. Cross strand C over strand B, then move strand C to the far left side *over* strand D. Move strand B to the far right side, *over* strand A.

13. Repeat steps 8 to 13 until the braid measures about 6½", leaving a little space between each full square knot.

14. Grouping all the loose strands together, make a large knot at the bottom of the braid. Thread each loose strand through a needle in turn and wrap it around the knot, pushing the needle through the knot to secure the strands. Try to achieve a nice round shape, then trim off any loose strands.

15. Repeat steps 7 to 12 to complete the second braid. Separate the strands, pushing two to the right and two to the left. Thread a needle with matching color thread, then make a stitch through each pair of strands, tight up against the last square knot. Loop the loose strands around each other, stitching them together to secure the loop. Trim.

Complete

16. Sew the buttons to the necklace piece from Step 5.

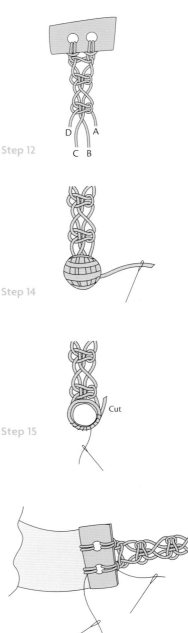

Step 12

Step 14

Step 15

Cut

Step 16

Periwinkle Pinwheel

When I was little, I could always spot a candy store by the spinning pinwheels displayed outside, their rods stuck into bales of straw. On blustery days, the colorful pinwheels would whistle in the wind, enticing children inside to buy sweets and candies. Festival booths would use pinwheels in the same way. Candy necklaces were among my favorite treats. Mint-flavored sweet powder was packed in 2" plastic tubes, which were tied together on a string. I would put my lips to one end of a tube and suck out a small amount of the powder as I walked around the festival grounds. The mint tasted cool and refreshing, and I felt very grown up to be wearing such an elegant necklace!

Make one flower

1. Cut two squares of fabric measuring 7¼" × 7¼". Follow the directions on page 8 to prepare the square for folding. Mark a 2¼" × 2¼" square at the center of each side. This is square A. The easiest way to do this is to fold the large square into thirds, first one way then the other, then press. The press lines are shown in the diagram on the next page.

Selections

Purse fabric: ⅛ yard or less of cotton or silk

Lining: ⅛ yard of less of cotton or silk

Handles: Cotton or silk scraps

Padding: ⅛ yard or less of felt

Leaves: Scraps of green patterned fabrics

Flower: Scraps of cotton or silk

Beads: 36 small round beads; 5 small bugle beads for flower; 16 large bugle beads for leaves; 1 large bead or button

#25 embroidery floss (6-ply)

⅛" cord: 1 yard

See template A on page 144. Use ¼" seam allowance for all sewing, unless otherwise indicated.

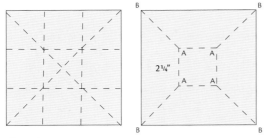

Step 2

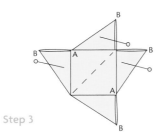

Step 3

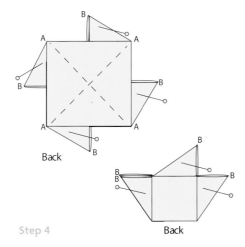

Back

Step 4

Back

2. Press carefully to create a firm fold along the edges of square A. Open out again. Lightly draw or press firmly diagonal lines as shown, from the outer corners of square A to each B corner of the sewn fabric square.

3. Put your finger firmly at the center of the smaller square, then fold inwards at the top AA line and the right-hand AA line, simultaneously. Tip B will rise to a triangular peak. Pin to hold. In the same way and still holding your finger firmly on the square base, push the bottom AA line inwards, creating a second peak. Pin as before. Repeat with the remaining sides of the small square. You now have a three-dimensional shape, with a square at the base.

4. Turn over, so that the square is at the top. Fold the square inwards along one of the diagonals shown. To do so, you will hold opposite B peaks in each hand and push toward the center. Note the boat shape that results.

5. Pick up the frontmost tip B as shown at the left of the diagram, and draw it downwards, again folding diagonally across the center square. The pinwheel shape shown here will result.

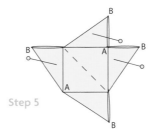

Step 5

6. Pick up top right corner A of the center square and fold it diagonally to bottom left corner A, revealing the inside fabric. Next, push the top left B tip upwards and to the right, resulting in the pinwheel shape shown. Fold then stitch all four B tips to the center front as shown.

7. Sew five small bugle beads in place to embellish the flower, as shown in the photograph.

Make the purse

8. Make a circle template measuring 5½" in diameter. Cut two from felt. Add ¼" seam allowance to the template (for a 6" diameter circle), then cut two from fabric for the front and back, plus two from lining fabric. Cut two strips of fabric measuring 1" × 18" for the piping (cut on the bias for extra stretch).

9. Fold in the seam allowances on the fabric pieces and press to hold. Slip a corresponding felt piece inside the folded-in seam allowance of each fabric piece. Sew the felt to the folded-in seam allowance, taking care not to let needle go through to the fabric front.

10. With leaf template A, cut six (three each from two different fabrics). Place two contrasting pieces right sides together, and sew around the perimeter, leaving about 1" open. Turn right side out, then sew the opening closed. Press. With embroidery thread, stitch through both layers of each leaf, making the vein pattern as shown. Begin with a single, long stitch

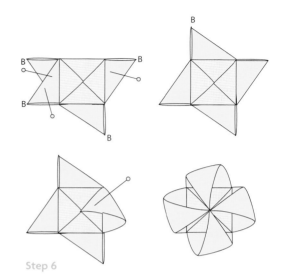

Step 6

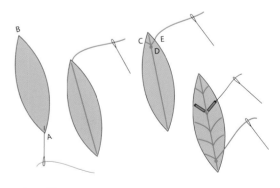

Step 10

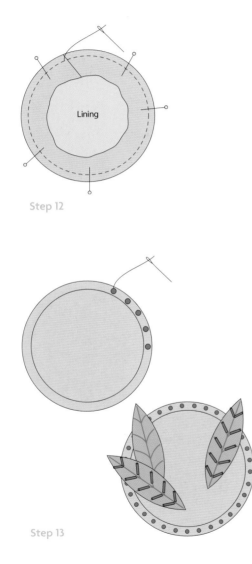

Step 12

Step 13

from the bottom (A) to the top (B) of the leaf; add ½"
diagonal stitches, starting at C, looping around the center
thread at D, and securing at E. Repeat down the length
of the first leaf. For the remaining two leaves, add bugle
beads to some of the ½"
diagonal stitches, as shown.

11. Using the lining circles from Step 7, turn under and
press a ¼" seam allowance. Pin the lining pieces to the
felt sides of the purse front and back. Working from the
lining side, use overstitch to sew each piece in place,
hiding the felt padding.

12. For the piping, fold one of the bias strips from step 7 in
half lengthwise, then press under a ¼" seam allowance
around all sides. Pin one long edge around the entire
perimeter of the lining side of the purse front, as shown.
Use a running stitch to sew in place. Wrap the other long
edge to the front side and stitch it in place as before. Repeat with the purse back.

13. Lining sides together, pin the purse front to the purse
back. Leaving about 6" open at the top, use a running
stitch to sew the front and back together, stitching as
close to the piping as possible. Sew 36 small round beads
onto the piping around the perimeter of the purse front,
spacing them equidistant. Arrange then sew the leaves
and flower onto the purse front.

Make the handle

14. Cut two strips of fabric measuring 1" × 13". Fold in half lengthwise and sew along the long raw edges, making two tubes. Turn right side out. Insert a length of ¼" cord through each tube, securing it at either end with two or three stitches. Twist the covered cords together, then sew the ends to either side of the opening at the top of the purse.

15. Cut two 1" circles of fabric. Turn the edges under by about ¼" around the perimeter, then sew in place to hide the ends of the handles.

Complete

16. Sew a decorative bead at the top center of the purse front. Make a button loop at the top center of the outside back of the purse. Begin by knotting two 8" strands of 6-ply embroidery floss together. Thread both strands through the same needle. Draw the needle from the inside back lining to the outside back, allowing the knot to sit tight against the inside back lining. Pin the knot to secure in place. Follow steps 9 to 10 of *Dandelion* on page 59 to complete the button loop.

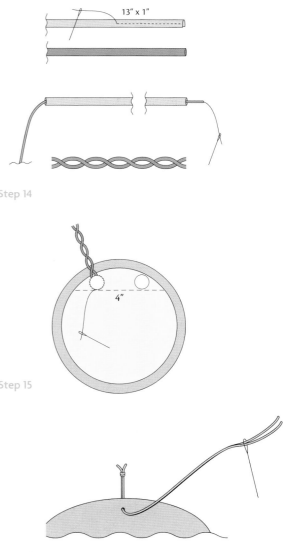

13" x 1"

Step 14

4"

Step 15

Step 16

A Little Girl Meets

Like everyone who looks back on a happy childhood, some of my favorite memories include sweets! One very special day, my brother and I happened to be in a candy store when the candy maker called by to deliver his goods. I was just four years old, but I remember this experience as clearly as though it happened yesterday.

In those days, when lucky children received an allowance, they would run to the corner shop or *dagashi-ya* to spend it. What an exciting time this was! The *dagashi-ya* would be filled with small thrills for children, everything from paper balloons and kites to small toys and, of course, candy.

That particular afternoon, I was lingering at the candy counter when I heard a bicycle bell outside. I ran to the doorway and watched as the candy sculptor turned the corner. On the back of his bicycle he had balanced a large wooden box. Greeted by a crowd of excited children, he jumped from his bicycle and slowly opened the lid. Inside, we saw a lump of thick, warm candy paste. The candy sculptor deftly nipped off a small ball of

paste and held it high for we children to see. He stretched and molded it with his clever fingers while it was still warm and pliable, then began snipping at it with a small clipper. Before our eyes, that lump of paste was transformed into an animal shape. A couple more pinches and the pricked ears of a fox emerged. Our magician dabbed at it with a paintbrush dipped in food coloring, adding color and texture. When he was finished, he stuck it on top of a stick and, with a flourish, handed it to a little child whose face glowed with pleasure.

"What do you want next?," he asked us. We yelled excitedly. "I want a dog!," "A raccoon, please!," "A rabbit!" A call for a crane and a nightingale quickly followed. The candy sculptor obliged, working his magic as he walked into the shop. Soon, the counter was filled with a color-

a Candy Sculptor

ful menagerie of creatures on candy sticks. As his audience of little children sighed with pleasure, he picked up a tiny monkey and attached a thin string, which he then twined around the stick. As he tugged at the string, the monkey came to life, climbing around and around its "tree."

But my favorite piece was a tiny bird, so sweet and pretty I could not help but stare at it. To make it, the candy sculptor had to knead the paste for a very long time, so that it was translucently thin and filled with air. When he was ready to start molding the shape, the paste looked completely white. After a few moments in his quick-moving hands, the bird began to take shape. He added a burst of yellow color to the chest and brushstrokes of green and pink to suggest wings. I watched as he poked a tiny hole through the beak and tail. He raised the bird to his lips and blew through

the hole. The tiny sweet trill of that candy nightingale rose through the air, filling the shop with joy.

When he was finished, the candy sculptor smiled and bowed to the crowd of mesmerized children, then made his exit. The show over, we children began to compete over pieces to buy. I tugged at my big brother's sleeve and whispered that I would like the nightingale. I walked home in a daze, whistling sweetly all the way. Back home, I blew and blew until the whistle finally failed. Then it was time for a tasty treat.

As I look back, my meeting with the candy sculptor has a dreamlike quality, but I know how very real and how happy this little event was. From watching him work his magic, I learned that beautiful things can be created from something as plain and shapeless as a lump of candy paste--or a swatch of fabric. Today, candy sculptors no longer amuse and delight children on street corners in Japan. I hope that my fond memories of their beautiful artwork will help rekindle some of the joy of those long lost days.

Butterfly Pin

蝶々飾り

I made this little butterfly pin from a prized member of my scarf collection, and so it has a long history. I wore the scarf on my first day of elementary school. That morning, I put on a dress my mother had made for me——a one-piece black velvet with a Peter-Pan collar. My sister picked up the red georgette scarf with its butterfly pattern and put it around my neck, like a tie. Then my father took a picture of me to commemorate the first day of my school life. His prized bonsai apple tree showed up beautifully beside me in the picture. Everything that happened on that morning was exciting to me, and I felt like a newly hatched butterfly setting off for a flower garden.

Make the butterfly

1. For the wings, cut rectangles in the following sizes from multi-colored fabrics (each includes ⅛" seam allowance).

   A and F, cut 4: 2" × 1"   E, cut 4: 4" × 1¾"
   B and H, cut 4: 3" × 1½"   G, cut 2: 2" × 1½"
   C and D, cut 4: 3½" × 1½"   I, cut 1: 3" × 1"

Selections

Butterfly fabric: **Colorful scraps**

#25 embroidery floss (6-ply)

Pin clasp (available from craft stores)

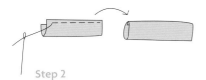

Step 2

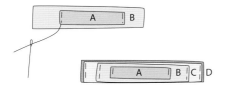

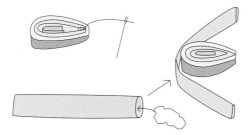

Step 3

2. Prepare wing pieces A, B, F, G, and two C pieces by folding each in half lengthwise, stitching along the long edges, and turning right side out to make "tubes." Press. Lay a very thin layer of same-size (or slightly smaller) batting on each of the two remaining C pieces and each E piece, then prepare in the same way as the other rectangles.

3. To make the upper wings, position A on top of B, stitching along the short ends to hold it in place. In the same way, stitch C on top of a padded D, then sew the A/B unit on top of the C/D unit. Fold the combined units in half lengthwise, with A on the inside, and stitch across the raw edges. Make two or three additional stitches across the top of the layers to hold them firmly in place. Wrap padded piece E around this unit and stitch across the raw edge as shown. Make two upper wings.

4. For the lower wings, repeat step 3, this time stitching F on top of G and a remaining G piece of top of H. As before, combine units, then fold and stitch across the raw edges. Make two lower wings. (Notice that this time there is no padded layer to wrap around the wing.)

5. Fold body piece I in half lengthwise. Sew around one short edge and the long edge to make a tube. Stuff as firmly as possible with batting scraps, then stitch the opening closed. Take a long strand of strong thread and

make a double stitch about ¼″ from the top of the tube. To form the butterfly's head, wrap the thread around the circumference of the tube, pull tight, then make another double stitch to hold. Repeat at ¼″ intervals down the rest of the tube, coiling the thread toward the tail end as shown. Double-stitch after each complete wrap. Exit the thread at the tip of the tail, then make three stitches up the front from coil to coil. After the last stitch, sink the needle into the body, then draw the thread back to the tail tip to exit. Do not cut the thread.

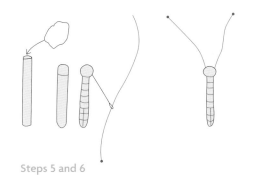

Steps 5 and 6

6. While there is still thread in the needle, poke the needle from the tail end along the full length of the body, exiting at the head, slightly right of center. Double stitch, then make a knot in the thread as close to the head as you can. Do not cut the thread. To form the antenna, make another knot about 2″ further down the thread. Repeat to make the second antenna, this time slightly left of the center of the head.

7. Sew each set of upper/lower wing pieces together, then join them as shown. Sew to the underside of the body.

Step 7

Complete

8. Sew a pin clasp to the back center of the butterfly.

Watermelon

西
瓜

Shakkei *is a Japanese landscaping techinique in which a garden is designed to incorporate the surrounding scenery, such as distant mountains or forest, as a beautiful background setting. It is loosely translated as "borrowed scenery." I often use a similar technique when selecting fabrics. For* Watermelon, *I chose a thick cotton drapery fabric with a large berry motif. I then made flowers from silks that harmonized with the first fabric. I positioned them on the purse so that, at first glance, they seemed to be part of the background. In this way, I created a three-dimensional scene, giving an illusion of depth. Careful placement of beads adds to the effect.*

Selections

Pouch fabric: ⅛ yard or less of cotton; silk scraps

Lining: ⅛ yard or less of cotton

Handle: Fabric scraps

Padding: Felt scraps

Flowers: ⅛ yard of less of silk

Beads: About 95 small beads

⅛" cord: 1 yard

See template A on on page 144. Use ½" seam allowance for purse pieces only; use ¼" seam allowance for other sewing.

Make two flowers

1. Cut two squares of fabric measuring 4 ⅜" × 4 ⅜", plus two more from a complementary fabric. Follow the directions on page 8 to prepare the squares for folding.

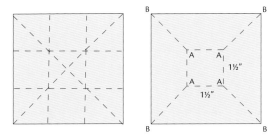

Step 2

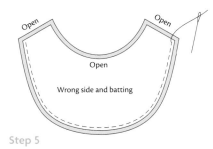
Step 5

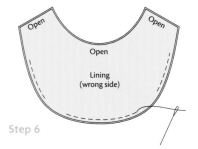
Step 6

2. Draw a 1½″ × 1½″ square at the center of each side. This is square A. Press carefully to create a firm fold along the edges of square A. Open out again. Draw diagonal lines as shown, from the outer corners of square A to each B corner of the sewn fabric square.

3. Follow steps 2 to 6 of *Periwinkle Pinwheel* on page 86 to 87 to make two smaller pinwheel flowers.

Make the pouch

4. With template A, cut two from batting. Add ½″ seam allowance to the template, then cut two from fabric for the purse front and back (be sure to place the template on the fold of the fabric before cutting). Cut two more for the purse lining. Baste the batting pieces to the wrong sides of the front and back. Trim the batting to a scant ⅛″ thickness. Sew the flowers in position on the purse front.

5. Right sides facing, sew the front to the back around the outer curve only. Leave the top and the handle sections open. Press the seam open. Turn under the seam allowances around the top and the handle sections, and press in place. Repeat with the lining pieces from step 4.

6. Wrong sides together, position the lining on top of the purse and pin in place, aligning the center bottom of the lining with the center bottom of the purse. Make a few small stitches through all layers at the center bottom to

secure the lining to the purse. Do the same at the right and left sides of the purse, as shown.

7. Turn the purse right side out, allowing the lining to fall in place inside. Neatly stitch the lining to the purse around the top curve, working from the lining side and stitching through the turned in seam allowances. Remove all basting stitches.

Make the handle

8. Cut two 1" × 9" strips of fabric. Fold each strip in half and, using a ¼" seam allowance, sew along the long edges to make a tube. Turn right side out. Thread a length of ⅛" diameter cord through each tube. Trim the cord to the same length as the tubes and secure each end with one or two stitches.

9. Make a few stitches to join the two tubes at the top, as shown. Gently twist the tubes around each other, and stitch them together at the other end to secure.

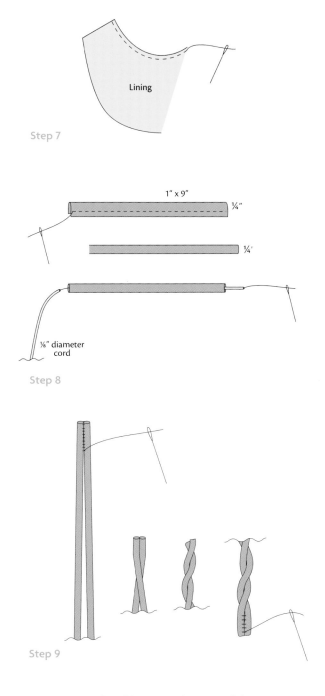

Step 7

Lining

Step 8

1" × 9"

¼"

¼'

⅛" diameter cord

Step 9

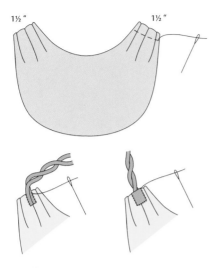

1½ " 1½ "

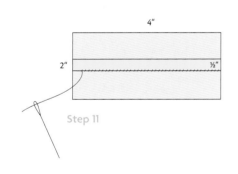

Step 10

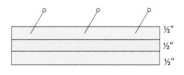

4"

2"   ½"

Step 11

                                      ½"
                                      ½"
                                      ½"

Step 12

10. Right side out, gather stitch across the top left and top right of the purse front. Pull the gathers until this measures about 1½" wide. Repeat with the purse back. Sew either end of the twisted handle to the inside right and left of the purse back, as shown. Cut two squares of lining fabric measuring 1" × 1". Fold in the raw edges and press. Pin the squares on top of the ends of the handle. Appliqué the first one in place, hiding the handle completely, as shown. Leave the second one unsewn for now.

11. Cut two strips of fabric measuring 2" × 4" and two strips of silk measuring 1" × 4". Turn under a ¼" seam allowance along the long edges of the 1" strip. Press. Pin then appliqué the narrow strip on top of the wider strip as shown.

12. Turn under a ¼" seam allowances along the long edges of the wide strip. Press and pin. Sew the short edges of the strip together to a tube. Turn right side out. Make a second tube in the same way.

13. Thread the handle through the first tube, then loop the tube over one of the front and back gathered sections of the purse top. Use overcast stitch to sew one edge in place, working around the entire front and back and encasing the handle, as shown. Gather-stitch around the other edge, then stuff the tube with batting scraps. Pull the thread tight to gather. Backstitch to hold.

14. Unpin the unstitched end of the handle from step 10. Loop the other tube in place, then attach as in step 11. Appliqué the unstitched appliqué square from step 10 in place.

Complete

15. If desired, cover a snap with lining fabric before sewing in place at the inside front and back.

16. Sting four sets of 15 small beads, and two sets of 12 beads. Sew each set in place as shown in the diagram, with two long strands and one short strand dangling from the handle at the purse front. If desired, embellish the purse front with a few more beads, as shown in the photograph.

Step 13

Step 15

Suzu Mari Handballs

Thoughts of my mother lie quietly at the bottom of my heart, but whenever I see traditional Japanese handballs, those memories spring to life. My mother dearly loved to sew and she kept even the smallest scraps of fabric in her sewing box. She would use them to make colorful handballs like these. Like my mother, I keep beautiful fabric scraps in a special box and I enjoy touching them in spare moments, even if I have no use for them in mind.

This easy-to-make handball has a bell inside; if you prefer you may stuff the bell box with potpourri to give the ball a sweet scent. Don't worry if the fabrics slip or shift while you are sewing; small irregularities add to the appeal of the finished ball.

Selections

Bell box: Stiff card or postcard, scotch tape

Core: Dollmaker's stuffing or fabric scraps, cotton scraps

Fabric: Scaps of colorful cottons or silks

Jingle bells or other noisemakers

See template A on page 145. Use ¼" seam allowance for all sewing.

Make the core

1. Make a small bell box by tracing template A on page 145 onto stiff card, then folding along the dashed lines. Put the bell or bells inside and seal the box with scotch tape.

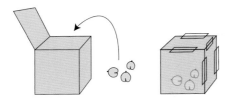

Step 1

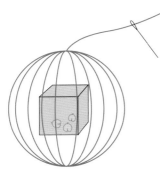

North pole

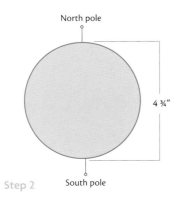

4 ¾"

Step 2   South pole

2. Begin by wrapping dollmaker's stuffing or fabric around the bell box. Wrap with lengths of stuffing until you have made a ball of about 4 ¾" diameter. Wrap the ball tightly with embroidery floss until you are able to create a nice, round shape. Roll the ball to make sure it is smooth and even. Keep wrapping until the ball rolls smoothly. Make a final wrap with a thin layer of fabric, stitching to hold in place as needed. Place pins to mark the top (north pole) and bottom (south pole) of the ball.

Cover the ball

3. Cut fabric to the following sizes:

Square A	1½" × 1½"	Cut 2
Rectangle B	1½" × 3"	Cut 6
Rectangle C	1¾" × 4½"	Cut 6
Rectangle D	1⅝" × 3"	Cut 6

4. Sew squares A to the north pole and south pole.

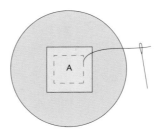

Step 4

5. Turn under a ¼″ seam allowance along one edge of each B rectangle and baste to hold. Follow the diagram to position three B rectangles in place at the north pole, creating a 1″ triangle at the center. Use a small overcast stitch to sew the turned-under edges of each B rectangle in place. Remove the basting stitches along this edge, then baste the opposite raw edge to the ball. Repeat at the south pole.

6. Repeat Step 5, this time adding the C rectangles as shown. Remove any remaining basting threads from Step 5.

7. Turn under a ¼″ seam allowance along all raw edges of rectangles D and baste. Pin the rectangles around the center of the ball, overlapping as shown. Use a small overcast stitch to sew in place. Remove all basting threads. If sections of your ball remain uncovered, continue cutting and placing rectangles as before until your ball is completely covered.

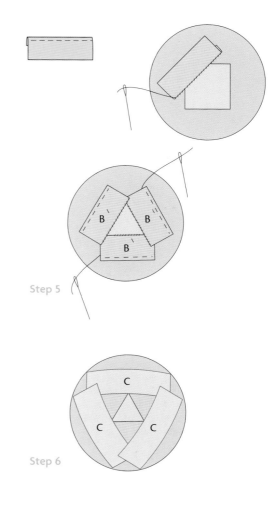

Step 5

Step 6

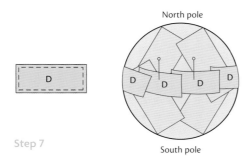

North pole

D

Step 7

South pole

Bell Fruit Charms

These tiny charms are inspired by memories of the soft handballs my mother would make for me as a child, as shown on page 102. Use them as you please on gift wrap, or as lamp pulls, key rings, or scissor fobs. The choice—and the daily pleasure they give—is yours. I like to add little touches like this to every gift I send. Long after the candy in the box is gone, your friends will enjoy this elegant hand-made gift tie.

Make a double yo-yo

1. Cut one circle measuring 2" and another measuring 2 ¼" in diameter. Fold in the raw edges by about ⅛" and press to hold. Gather stitch around the circumference, through the folded-in seam. Pull the gathers tight and backstitch. Press lightly. Make one or two stitches at the center to secure the smaller yo-yo on top of the larger one.

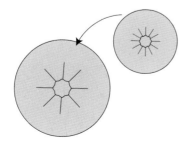

Step 1

Selections

Berry: Scraps

Yo-yos: Silk scraps

Stuffing: Batting or fabric scraps

⅛" ribbon: 10"

See template A on page 145. Use ⅛" seam allowance for all sewing.

Make the berry

2. With template A, cut five from fabric. Using a ⅛" seam allowance, sew the five pieces together lengthwise to form the berry shape, leaving the top open. Fold the top seam allowance inwards and finger-press to hold. Stuff firmly with cotton batting or fabric scraps.

3. Gather-stitch around the top of the berry, through the folded-in seam allowance. Pull the gathers tight, trapping the batting inside, then stitch to secure. Do not cut the thread yet.

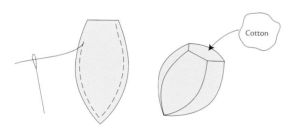

Cotton

Step 2

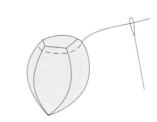

Step 3

Complete

4. Use the same thread to stitch the double yo-yo on top of the berry.

5. Make a small knot at either end of the ribbon, then fold it in half. Stuff the knots inside the top-most yo-yo and stitch to secure.

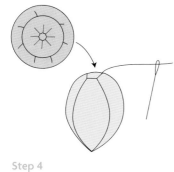

Step 4

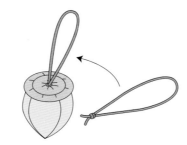

Step 5

Yokan

Fun, colorful, and deliciously sweet, *yokan wagashi*

are a favorite among Japanese children. These soft

jellies might be molded into a flower, a fish, a bird

or any number of playful shapes. Delightful to hold,

they melt on the tongue then burst into fruity flavors.

The projects in this chapter are similarly playful. Like

yokan candies, each one brings to mind a sweet

childhood memory.

Candy Cache

飴玉

In its design and colors, this little purse is inspired by the sweetest of childhood memories. The bright leaves and the brilliant orange beneath are meant to resemble colorful candy drops spilling from a pretty tin can. They are made from the silk lining of a kimono, while the pouch itself is cotton. I used wooden beads from an old necklace for the little round candies. The handle is made from a silk scarf and it reminds me of ribbon bows that my mother would tie in my hair.

Make the purse

1. With template A, cut two from felt. Add ½″ seam allowance to the template, then cut two from fabric for the front and back, plus two from lining fabric. With template B, cut one from silk.

Selections

Purse fabric: ⅛ yard or less of cotton

Leaves and orange print: ⅛ yard of less of silk

Padding: ⅛ yard or less of felt

Beads: 10 colorful candy-size beads; 1 larger bead or button; 2 large and six small round beads for handles

2 ½″ ribbon: About 2 ¾ yards

#25 embroidery floss (6-ply)

Hair elastic loop

See templates A to C on on pages 146 to 147. Use ½″ seam allowance for purse pieces only; use ¼″ seam allowance for other sewing.

Back view

Felt

Step 2

2. Fold in the seam allowances on purse pieces A and press to hold. Slip a corresponding felt piece inside the folded-in seam allowances. Sew the felt to the folded-in seam allowance, taking care not to let needle go through to the fabric front.

3. With template C, cut six leaves. Turn in a ¼″ seam allowance, then press and baste to hold. Appliqué the leaves in place onto the template B fabric from step 1. Appliqué in sequence from leaf 1 to leaf 5, overlapping as shown. Turn in a ⅛″ seam allowance around the entire perimeter of the template C fabric, then press and baste. Appliqué this piece, with five leaves attached, to the purse front. Appliqué the remaining leaf to the purse back. Remove all basting threads.

4. Using the lining pieces A from Step 1, turn under and press a ½″ seam allowance. Pin the lining pieces to the felt sides of the purse front and back. Working from the lining side, use overstitch to sew each piece in place, hiding the felt padding.

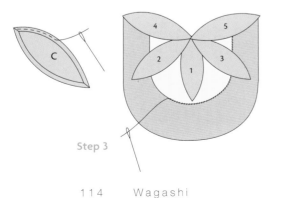

Step 3

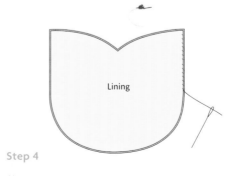

Lining

Step 4

5. Using a 2-ply strand of embroidery thread and herringbone stitch (see page 13), sew the front and back together, leaving the top open. Using the photograph as a guide, stitch a decorative button to the center top of the purse front. Stitch the candy-style beads in place, saving one for the purse back.

Make the handle

6. Angle-cut the ribbon into two 15" lengths. Double-fold a ⅛" hem around all edges of the ribbon and stitch in place.

7. Sew a ribbon to each side of the purse, stitching about ½" from the purse top and allowing about 1½" of ribbon to hang loose. Sew beads as desired over the stitches. Tie the ribbons loosely together to create the handle.

Complete

8. Use a 2 " diameter hair elastic as a button loop. Alternatively, follow steps 9 to 10 of *Dandelion* (see page 59) to make a loop from embroidery floss. Cut a 1" square of fabric. Turn under and press a ¼" seam allowance around all sides. Wrap the square around the loop twice, then sew it to the inside back of the purse, securing the loop in place.

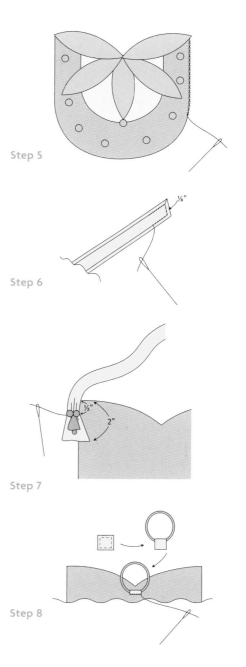

Step 5

Step 6

Step 7

Step 8

Evening Primrose

This charming hair tie was actually designed first as a bracelet, which you will see when you turn to the next page. The braiding is simple and is done in the same way as Hana-no-en *on page 34, but my bracelet features a different flower design. Of course, you may substitute any flower you wish for the one I have chosen. I love the gentle curves and the three-dimensional quality of* Evening Primrose, *and the beads add extra sparkle. I used the same flower design to create the pretty prom corsage and the key fob photographed on pages 120 and 121. Once you begin making flower designs, you will be surprised how many ways you can use them! The three short projects that follow are photographed in various different styles so that you can see just how versatile little flower designs like this one can be.*

月見草

Selections

Flower: **Cotton scraps**

Beads: **About 20 delica beads per flower**

#25 embroidery floss (6-ply): **Selection of colors (for bracelet only)**

1 ½" wired ribbon: **1 yard (for wrist corsage only)**

Hook and eye (for wrist corsage only)

Stuffing: **Batting scraps (for key fob only)**

Novelty yarn or ⅛" ribbon (for key fob only)

Key ring (for key fob only): **Available from craft stores**

Bracelet

For the braiding, I used a multi-colored cord. If you prefer more distinct color in your braid, you can use different colored cords to achieve the effect shown in the diagrams.

Make one flower

1. Make a circle template measuring 3 ⅛" in diameter. Cut one each of two different fabrics. Follow the directions on page 8 to prepare the circles for folding. Lightly mark the center point on each side.

2. Make four inward folds as shown, each about ½" at its midpoint. Pin and press. Make one or two stitches at each corner to hold. You now have a perfect square.

3. Turn over, then fold each corner back to the center point marked in step 1. Pin and press, making another perfect square. Make one or two stitches about ½" from the center point, stitching through all layers, as shown.

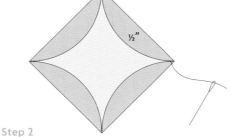

Step 2

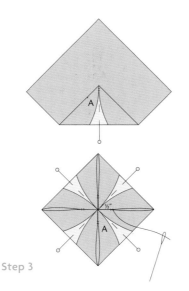

Step 3

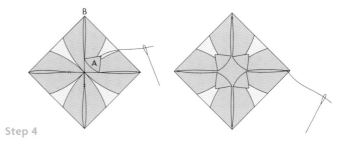

Step 4

4. Fold each tip A back on itself again, making a fold at the previous stitch marks. A perfect square will form at the center.

5. Fold tip B forward toward the center square, stitching in place as shown. Stitch delica beads as desired to the center square.

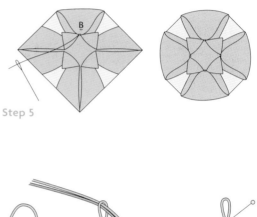

Step 5

Weave the cord

6. Cut three lengths of cord, novelty yarn or embroidery floss measuring 85". Fold all three strands in half. Make a ½" loop at the midpoint of one of them, knotting as shown. Loop the other two strands through the loop, pinning the midpoints and the base of the loop to a firm pincushion. You now have six strands to work with. Follow steps 6 to 10 of *Hana-no-en* on pages 37 to 38 to make a 7" bracelet.

7. At the bottom, make a large knot with all strands together, stitching or gluing the loose strands in place to avoid fraying. Sew the completed flower to the center of the bracelet braid.

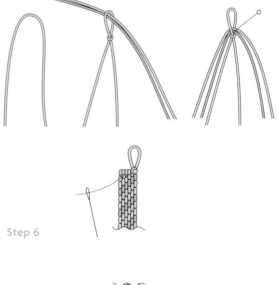

Step 6

Step 7

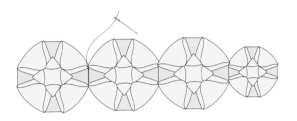

Step 4

Step 5

Wrist Corsage

Made with pretty wired ribbon, this project is perfect for the prom or any special occasion.

Make four flowers

1. Make a circle template measuring 4½". Cut three circles from each of two contrasting fabrics. Follow the directions on page 8 to prepare the circles for folding.
2. Following Steps 2 to 5 on page 118, make three large flowers. Make one small flower using the 3⅛" template from *Evening Primrose Bracelet*.
3. Cut three 1¾" circles from felt. Sew the felt circles to the backs of the large flowers to add extra firmness.
4. Use overcast stitch to sew the three large flowers together in a row. Add the small flower to one end of the row.

Make four ribbon fans

5. Cut four 6" lengths of 1½" wide wired ribbon. Turn each short edge inwards twice by about ¼" each time, and hem securely. Make six or seven evenly-spaced pleats along the length of each ribbon. Gather-stitch along one long edge, pull the gathers tight, then stitch to hold. You will now have four fan-shaped pieces of ribbon.
6. Sew the ribbon fans to the back of the corsage, positioning them between the large flowers as in the photograph.
7. Attach a hook and eye at either end of the corsage to fasten.

Key Fob

Two flowers from different fabrics, sewn back to back—what could be simpler?

Make two flowers

1. Using the 4 ¼" template from *Evening Primrose Wrist Corsage*, cut three circles from each of two contrasting fabrics. Follow the directions on page 8 to prepare the circles for folding.
2. Following Steps 2 to 5 on page 118, make two flowers

Complete

3. As desired, string three short lengths of embroidery floss with delica beads, ending each with a larger decorative bead. Stitch them to the back of one of the flowers, center bottom, allowing them to dangle.
4. Cut 15 strands of ribbon or novelty yarn, varying the lengths from 6" to 7". Stitch them to the back of the flower, as before. Sew the key ring to the top center of the same flower.
5. Position the flowers with wrong sides together and pin to hold. Use overcast stitch to sew them together around the perimeter, leaving about 1" open. Stuff with cotton batting, then sew the opening closed.

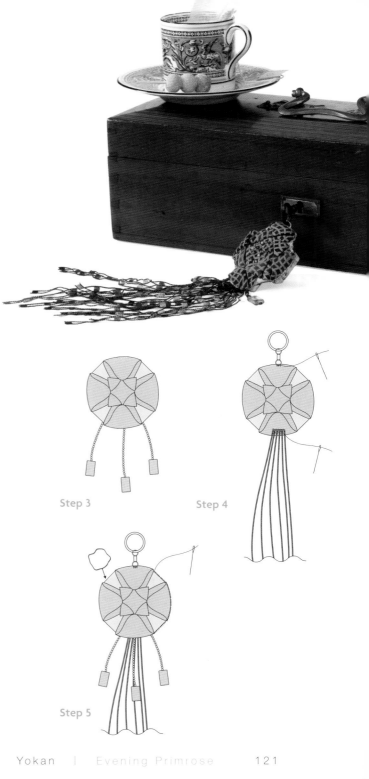

Step 3

Step 4

Step 5

Candy Drops: Sweet

Like a candy maker sculpting plain paste into sweet delicacies, I, too, seek to transform the everyday into something to be cherished. My fabric creations are inspired by simple memories from my childhood.

I was born in Tokyo and spent my first eight years in the city. I then moved to the mountainous district of Kamakura to live with my aunt, whose home was a shrine deep in the forest. In this beautiful setting, I discovered many of the marvels of nature, and each one—no matter how small—would make my heart jump with joy.

When I was twelve, I moved again, this time to a house near the ocean. Not long after my arrival, a classmate, perhaps sensing my loneliness, invited me to the beach which was just minutes away. It was a misty day, with a light rain. My new friend watched me walk slowly toward the ocean. In an almost philosophical tone, she said to me, "Kumiko, lie down and turn yourself into sand. I will turn into ocean waves and wash away all your suffering for you." She then showed me how to search the shallows for sea-glass left behind by the receding tides. In lovely shades of blues and greens, these were true treasures to our young eyes. Once in a while, the memory of those moments still passes through my heart like a piece of poetry. From then on, I would spend as much time as I could at the beach. As soon as I got home from school, I would drop my satchel and head for the sands. Rather than play in the water, I would spend my time hunting for unusual pebbles, sea shells, interesting plants, or even seaweed and the tiny creatures that live among it. I always came home with a treasure or two.

I loved to walk through the big pine forest that brushed up against the ocean. I was always certain that something interesting was wait-

Memories of Childhood

ing there for me. One day I might stumble across dozens of cute, egg-shaped white mushrooms peeking out from a bed of pine needles. Another day, I would happen upon a patch of bright yellow mushrooms with brown spongy caps. As I crept toward them, I would imagine the mushrooms were pixies, beckoning me into their fantasy forest. I would look up though the tall pines into an endless blue sky, watching cotton-candy clouds smile down at me. How time would fly as I walked through the forest, my own private kingdom under a canopy of green.

Stepping out of my forest and back onto the beach, my feet would sink pleasantly into the soft sand. I enjoyed the feeling that my body was blending into the natural world. I would notice the sunlight on the water and stop a moment to watch the waves splash over my feet then disappear quietly into the sand, leaving bright saltwater bubbles behind. Sometimes, the bubbles would pop to reveal beautiful pieces of sea-glass that had been carried in on the waves. With a cry of joy, I would pick them up and spread them out on my palms. Having tumbled for months or years among the sand and waves, they had lost their jagged edges and were as smooth and round as fine gems. One day, before I knew what I was doing, I popped one into my mouth as though it were a candy drop. I remember a faint taste of salt and seaweed filled my mouth as I stood there in the gently singing wind.

Like sea-glass, all these experiences have become my treasures. As I hold a piece of fabric in my hands, my memories inspire me. Just as a candy maker sculpts delicate *wagashi* from *azuki* paste, I make my own sweet things out of special moments that have so enriched my life. My towns, my mountains, my ocean, and my friends . . . all are there at the tips of my fingers, ready to be molded into shapes anew.

Malipoense Pouch

マリポエンセ

One afternoon, my sisters and I took a walk in the mountains after a rainfall. We happened across a pocket of flowers, moistened by raindrops. They were so pretty I wanted to take them home. Yet I hesitated, since the flowers seemed to be holding a lot of dreams inside and I did not want to disturb them. I carried them home in my memory instead.

Today, combining fabrics in blue and lime, I tried to recreate that long-ago image of malipoenses——or jade slipper orchids—growing quietly and peacefully among the trees. Enjoy choosing beads that complement the colors you selected for the purse. I varied the sizes and colors of my beads to accentuate the motifs in fabric I used.

Selections

Pouch fabric: ⅛ yard or less of cotton or silk

Lining: Felt in contrast color

Flower: Scrap of cotton or silk

Beads: 4 large beads; 4 mid-size beads; 3 small beads; about 25 delica beads

Decorative cord: About 2 ¾ yards

#25 embroidery floss (6-ply)

See templates A and B on on page 148. Use ½" seam allowance for purse pieces only; use ¼" seam allowance for other sewing.

Make one flower

1. Make a circle template measuring 3 ½″ in diameter. Cut two circles (each from a different fabric). Follow the directions on page 8 to prepare the circles for folding. Cut a strip of felt measuring ¾″ × 10″ and a strip of fabric measuring 2″ × 10½″.

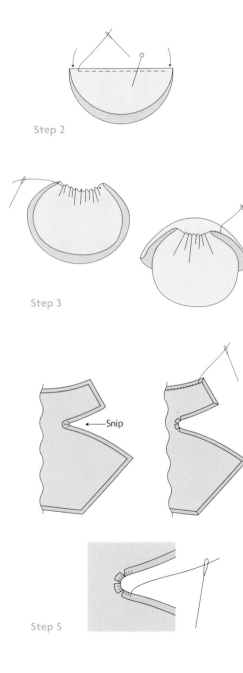

Step 2

Step 3

Step 5

Snip

2. Fold the flower piece in half, then slide the top half back by about ³⁄₈". Press. Gather-stitch through all layers along the folded edge, leaving about ¼" at either end.

3. Pull the gathers tight and make three or four stitches to hold. Fold back the bottom layer as shown, and add a few at either side to hold the layers in place.

Make the pouch

4. With templates A and B, cut two each from felt. Add ½" seam allowance to the templates, then cut one each from fabric for the front and back. Cut a strip of felt measuring ⁵⁄₈" × 9¾", and a strip of fabric measuring 1¾" × 10¾".

5. Fold in the seam allowances on fabric pieces A and B and press to hold. Slip a corresponding felt piece inside the folded-in seam allowance of fabric pieces A and B. Sew the felt to the folded-in seam allowance, taking care not to let the needle go through to the fabric front. On piece B, snip the tight curve as shown to allow the curve to lie flat. Reinforce both curves with buttonhole stitch.

6. Position the remaining felt A and B pieces over the felt sides of the front and back. Sew in place, hiding the turned-in seam allowance.

7. Fold in a ¼" seam allowance around all sides of the fabric strip from Step 1. Wrap the felt strip inside, then use a small overstitch to sew closed.

8. Beginning at the top right, position then pin the covered strip in place along the edge of the pouch front. Wrap around the right side, bottom, and left side of the pouch. Use a 2-ply strand of embroidery floss and herringbone stitch (see page 13), worked from the pouch front, to sew the strip in place. Repeat, this time wrapping the other side of the strip around the right side, bottom, and left side of the pouch back.

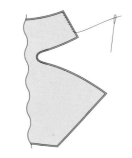

Step 6

Make two handles

9. For each braided handle, cut two 37" lengths of cord (total of four). Fold in half, marking the midpoints with pins. Pin the midpoints of two cords to a firm pincushion. You will now have four working strands of cord, A to D. Follow steps 8 to 13 of *Purple Dianthus* on pages 82 to 83 to make two braided handles.

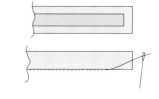

Step 7

Complete

10. Fold each end of first handle over by about ½" and sew to the inside of the purse, at either side of the front flap. Repeat with the second handle, sewing to the inside back.Sew a snap or a Velcro tab below the flap to close.

11. Sew the flower to the center of the pouch flap, with the top of the flower resting about ½" from the top of the flap. Embellish the flap with beads.

Hagoromo

羽
衣

This lovely pincushion doubles as a paperweight. A hagoromo is an extremely delicate cloth made of feathers. It is worn by tennyo— mythical Japanese ladies who are equivalent to angels in Western culture. Hagoromo is also the title of a famous Noh drama, which I remember watching from the front row as a child. The story tells of a tennyo who flies from the sky and hangs a beautiful hagoromo on a pine branch as she strolls the beach nearby. A fisherman finds it and, fascinated by its unearthly beauty, decides to take it home. The tennyo, dismayed at her loss, begs the fisherman to return her treasured cloak to her. He returns it and watches her fly away, her magical hagoromo dancing enchantingly behind her.

There is variety of sweet candy or wagashi known as hagoromo. Its light pink color inspired my pincushion design.

Selections

Pincushion cover: **Cotton scraps in rich florals**

Padding: **Felt scraps**

Stuffing: **Batting or fabric scraps**

Yo-yo: **Silk or cotton scrap**

Beads: **9 small round beads; 6 bugle beads;**

   12 delica beads

See template A to D on page 149. Use ¼" seam allowance for all sewing.

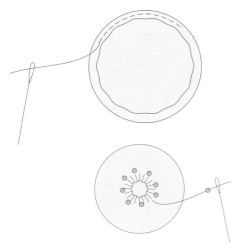

Step 1

Step 4

Make a yo-yo

1. Cut a circle of fabric measuring 3" diameter. Fold in the raw edge by about ¼" and press to hold. Gather stitch around the circumference, through the folded-in seam. Pull the gathers tight and backstitch. Press lightly. Sew six decorative beads around the circumference of the yo-yo.

Make the pincushion

2. Make a circle template measuring 4¼" diameter. Cut 3 from felt. Add ¼" seam allowance to the template (making a 4¾" circle), then cut one from fabric for the bottom of the pincushion. Cut a strip of felt measuring ¾" × 12¾" and a strip of fabric measuring 1¼" × 13¼".

3. Fold in a ¼" seam allowance on the fabric circle from step 2, then press to hold. Slip a felt circle inside the folded-in seam allowance. Sew the felt to the folded-in seam allowance, taking care not to let needle go through to the fabric front. Sew a second circle of felt to the first, hiding the folded-in seam allowance. Trim the second circle slightly.

4. Wrap the felt strip from step 2 inside the fabric strip and sew to hold, as shown.

5. Using diamond template A, cut three. Take care to center any floral pattern on the template. Right sides together, use a running stitch to sew two pieces together along one long

edge. Set in the third piece, forming a hexagon out of the three diamonds. Take care to sew neatly from angle to angle. Turn under the remaining raw edges by ¼". Sew a decorative bead to the center of each diamond.

Step 5

6. Appliqué the three-piece unit from step 5 onto the remaining circle of felt. Thread a needle with an 18" length of embroidery floss and knot. Inserting from back to front, come up at the outer angle where two diamonds join. Thread a delica, a bugle bead, and a second delica, allowing them to lie along the edge of the pieced diamond. Make a stitch into the felt to secure. Come up again about 1" away, and thread a second set of delica-bugle-delica, this time securing at the next outer angle. Repeat around the perimeter of the pieced diamonds, securing a total of six bead sets (two per diamond).

7. Pin a long edge of the fabric covered felt strip from step 4 evenly around the circumference of the pincushion top from step 6. Use a two-ply strand of embroidery floss and herringbone stitch to attach the strip, removing pins as you go. When the two ends of the strip meet, use overcast stitch to sew them together. Repeat, this time sewing the remaining long edge of the strip to the pincushion base. Before closing, stuff firmly with batting or cotton scraps.

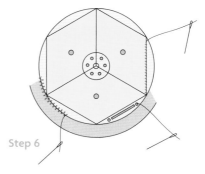

Step 6

Nimble Thimbles

These pretty thimbles will protect your fingers while adding a splash of color to your sewing box. They are made from a double layer of felt, and can be embellished any way you wish. I used bright colors so that I can easily find a thimble when I need one! Keep a few in your sewing room, more in your sew-and-go bag.

Fabric thimbles make great gifts for children, too. Better still, combine your gift with a quick sewing lesson by giving one completed thimble and the makings for a second. Little projects like this are a very good introduction to sewing for young children.

Make a thimble

1. Using template A, cut a thimble from felt. Fold the piece in half along the dotted line, as shown. Using overcast stitch, sew from A to B, securing at B with a double stitch. Push from the base to create a *y* shape as shown, and sew both short seams. Turn right side out.

Selections

Thimble: Felt scraps

Trim: Cotton or silk scraps for trim

Beads: 21 delica beads per thimble

See template A on page 149. Use ⅛" seam allowance for all sewing.

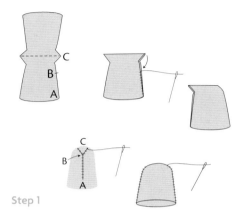

2. Cut a strip of fabric measuring ¾" × 3". Position it right sides around the top edge of the thimble. Using an ⅛" seam allowance, sew the trim in place around the circumference of the thimble. Open out the seam. Turn the other long edge and the short ends inwards by ⅛" and press to hold. Appliqué in place around the inside circumference of the thimble.

Complete

3. Make three beaded daisies, as shown. First, sew the center bead in place, then string and sew six beads evenly around it.

Templates

All templates are drawn to full size and do not include seam allowances, unless specified otherwise. You will find that for many projects you will need to cut the same shape first from felt and then from fabric. Begin by tracing or photocopying the template onto template plastic or stiff card. Transfer all labels and markings. Using tailor's chalk or another quilters' marker, lightly draw around the template, then cut the felt pieces you need. Next, eyeball the correct seam allowance—usually ¼" or ⅛", as indicated on the template. Draw around the template, directly onto your fabric, adding that seam allowance in. If you are uncomfortable estimating the seam allowance, remake your templates on a new sheet of template plastic or card, this time with the seam allowance already added in. Remember that sewing is very forgiving—if your seam allowance is slightly off, it will not be noticeable on the finished piece.

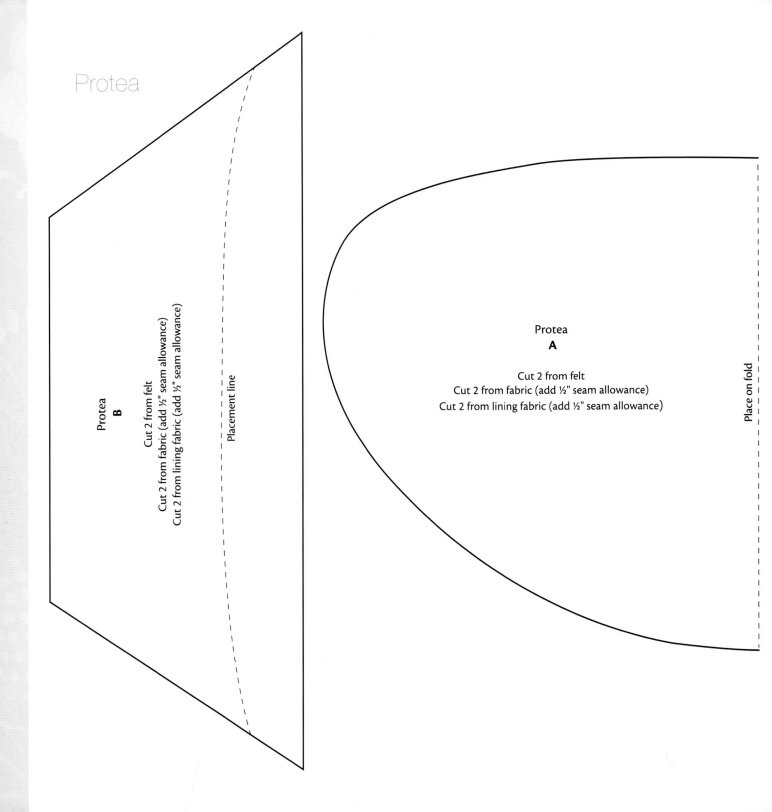

Protea

B

Cut 2 from felt
Cut 2 from fabric (add ½" seam allowance)
Cut 2 from lining fabric (add ½" seam allowance)

Placement line

Protea
A

Cut 2 from felt
Cut 2 from fabric (add ½" seam allowance)
Cut 2 from lining fabric (add ½" seam allowance)

Place on fold

Protea

Bugaku Drum

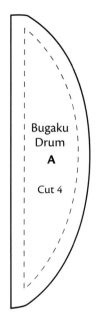

Bugaku
Drum
A

Cut 4

Hana-no-en

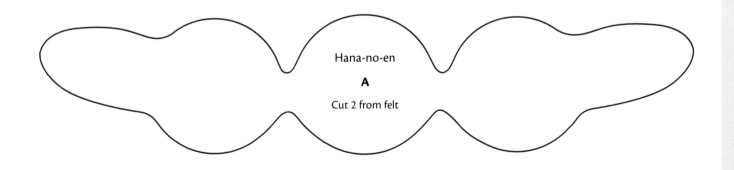

Hana-no-en

A

Cut 2 from felt

Berry, Berry

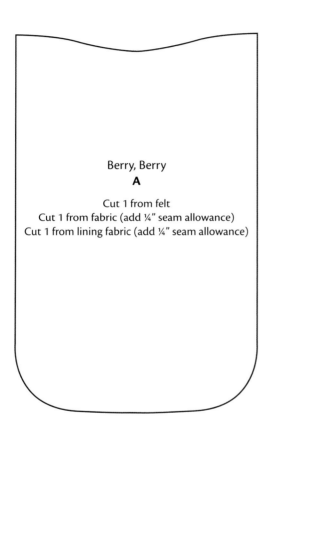

Berry, Berry
A

Cut 1 from felt
Cut 1 from fabric (add ¼" seam allowance)
Cut 1 from lining fabric (add ¼" seam allowance)

Berry, Berry
B

Cut 1 from felt
Cut 1 from fabric (add ¼" seam allowance)
Cut 1 from lining fabric (add ¼" seam allowance)

Berry, Berry

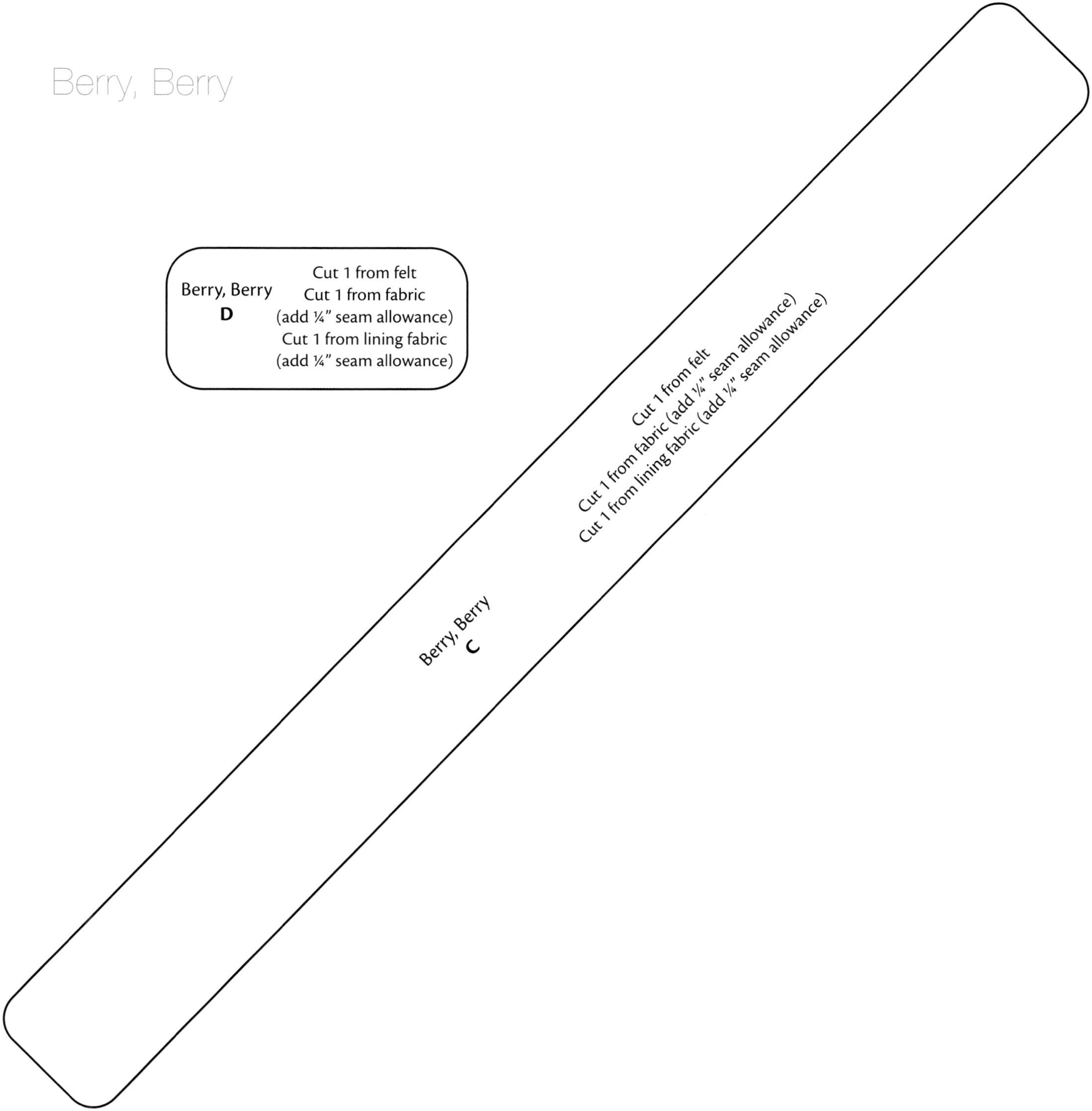

Berry, Berry
D

Cut 1 from felt
Cut 1 from fabric
(add ¼" seam allowance)
Cut 1 from lining fabric
(add ¼" seam allowance)

Cut 1 from felt
Cut 1 from fabric (add ¼" seam allowance)
Cut 1 from lining fabric (add ¼" seam allowance)

Berry, Berry
C

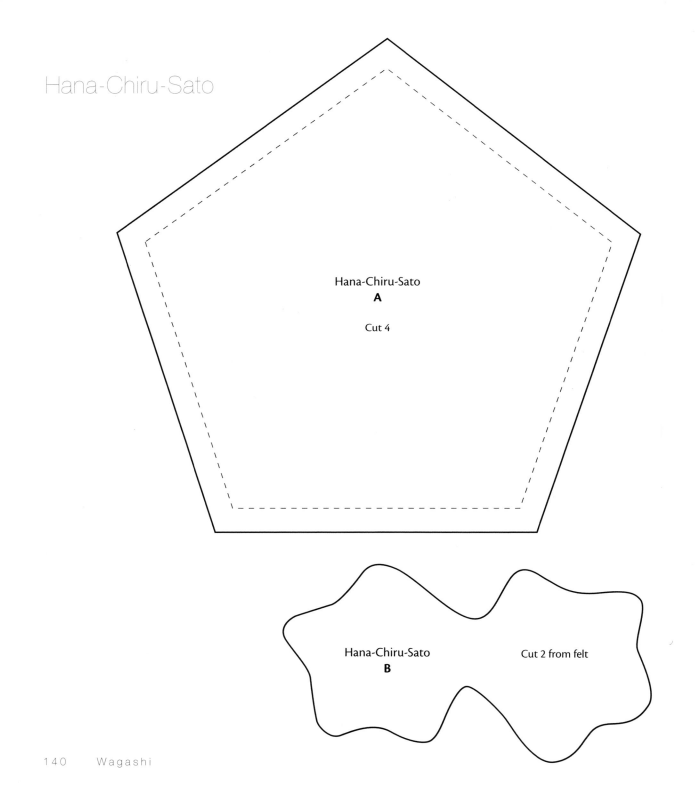

Hana-Chiru-Sato

Hana-Chiru-Sato
A

Cut 4

Hana-Chiru-Sato
B

Cut 2 from felt